W9-BPJ-711

OPEN *house*

A Culinary Tour

The Junior League of Murfreesboro

To Darlene -
Enjoy!
Love,
Gail

OPEN
house
A Culinary Tour

The Junior League of Murfreesboro
P. O. Box 4138
Murfreesboro, Tennessee 37133
www.JLMurfreesboro.org

Copyright © 2002 by
The Junior League of Murfreesboro

ISBN: 0-9716711-0-9
Library of Congress Number: 2002102880

Edited, Designed, and Manufactured by
Favorite Recipes Press®, an imprint of

P. O. Box 305142
Nashville, Tennessee 37230
800-358-0560

Book Design: Starletta Polster
Art Director: Steve Newman
Project Editor: Ginger Dawson

Manufactured in the United States of America
First Printing: 2002
10,000 copies

THE JUNIOR LEAGUE OF MURFREESBORO

In February 1992, a dedicated group of twenty-four Murfreesboro women came together to explore and develop an organization which would provide an infrastructure for our growing numbers of willing volunteers.

The chosen organization was the Association of Junior Leagues International and under the development of President Anne Davis, the group began to follow the AJLI blueprint for development.

Four months after the initial meeting on May 10, 1992, The Junior Service League of Murfreesboro was incorporated. Throughout the year, plans were made for the first provisional class of 100 women, fund-raising occurred, and training began on volunteer and community-related topics.

In May 1993, the first provisional class became "actives" and set out in placements throughout the community, many of which continue to the present. In 1995, The Junior Service League of Murfreesboro officially became a Junior League, in record time for the fulfillment of tasks necessary. As The Junior League of Murfreesboro celebrates its tenth year, our community continues to reap the benefits of this group's focused and sincere endeavors. Twenty-four women began a decade of "strengthening the community, one child at a time." We owe these women our sincere gratitude.

Betty Childress	Susan Loyd
Kim Cleveland	Patty Marschel
Cecil Coleman	Charlotte McKnight
Debbie Cope	Mary Dodd Mifflin
Anne Davis	Kitty Murfree
Melinda Haines	Marilyn Newsom
Alicia Hollis	Kit Ramsay
Kathy Hoover	Sarah Ridley Piggens
Ginger Ingle	Doris Sawyer
Susan Kane	Mary Spence Francis
Melinda Keisling	Barbara Sutton
Billie Little	Marimae White

VISION OF
THE JUNIOR
LEAGUE OF
MURFREESBORO

*A diverse group
of women
building a better
community through
a commitment to
advocacy, leadership,
multiculturalism
and commitment
to children.*

*Strengthening the
community,
one child at a time.*

COOKBOOK COMMITTEE

MISSION

The Junior League of Murfreesboro is an organization of women committed to promoting voluntarism and to improving the community through the effective action and leadership of trained volunteers. Its purpose is exclusively educational and charitable. The Junior League of Murfreesboro reaches out to women of all races, religions and national origins who demonstrate an interest in and commitment to voluntarism.

Co-Chair–KRISTIN RYAN

Co-Chair–JANET LEE

Recipe Chair–PRISCILLA JACKSON

Recipe Co-Chair–AMANDA HALES

Art and Design Chair–CHERYL TERRY

Non-Recipe Text Chair–JULIE DILIBERTI

Non-Recipe Text Co-Chair–LESLIE AKINS

Marketing Chair–JANA ROGERS

Marketing Co-Chair–KAREN CARNES

Often a cook has a secret ingredient that makes a good meal great. The Cookbook Committee wishes to extend our gratitude to the following individuals whose contributions helped make our book that much better:

LYNN JACOBS–*Creation of the Children's Chapter*

MITZI MICHAELSON–*Procurement of Cover Artwork*

GREG NICHOLSON–*Line Art Contribution*

LEANNA WRIGHT–*Board Member Liaison*

ACKNOWLEDGMENTS

About the Artist… Henry Barnes is originally from Union Point, Georgia. After attending college on an athletic scholarship, he pursued several different careers before settling on his career as an artist. He has studied intensively at the Chatov Studio. He went to Paris in 1983 and studied with noted French artist Yves Brayer. His works are represented in collections throughout Georgia and the Southeast. We are honored and thankful to have a representation of his work for our cookbook cover.

About the Photographer… All of the elegant photographs of the homes are the work of photographer Jack Ross. Contributing not only his talent but also much of his time, the cookbook is significantly enhanced by the quality of his efforts. Jack Ross is a native Tennessean who has lived in Murfreesboro since 1975. He is the director of Photographic Services at Middle Tennessee State University. Previous published works include his work with author Terry Weeks, *Heart of Tennessee, The Story and Images of Historic Rutherford County.* Jack is heavily involved in community activities and also is a free-lance photographer; he has photographed thousands of images in and around Middle Tennessee. His tremendous talent is obvious and the League is privileged and deeply appreciative of his contributions.

The Peddler… Many of the decorative accessories appearing in our photographs were graciously lent to the League by The Peddler. Well known for their fine gifts, antiques, bridal registry, and stationery, The Peddler has been a part of Murfreesboro for over 30 years. We extend our heartfelt thanks to owners Jane Jones and Mary Ann Richardson.

Henry's Florist… The beautiful flower arrangements shown in our photographs are all the creations of Henry Philips. Owner and operator of Henry's Florist for over 20 years, Mr. Philips is known in Murfreesboro for specializing in European design. Receiving imported flowers from Holland on a weekly basis, his exotic flowers and elegant arrangements make every occasion special. The beauty of his work speaks for itself in our photographs and the League is sincerely grateful for his time and creative efforts.

TABLE OF

contents

You are invited to an OPEN HOUSE...

In the South,

our entertaining is legendary,

and as we begin our

culinary tour of Middle Tennessee,

you will see why.

Our inviting homes are merely a backdrop

for our delicious food,

and our beautiful table settings

are mere instruments to help

us enjoy what the hostess has prepared.

The food and décor help to

make the coming together of friends

that much more special.

As we open our homes to you,

sit back and enjoy—

the party is just beginning...

WEEKEND
brunch

MIXED FRUIT GRANOLA WITH VANILLA YOGURT

TENNESSEE SPICE MUFFINS

LEMON POPPY SEED SCONES

SAUSAGE STRATA

FRESH VEGETABLE FRITTATA

CHEDDAR GRITS SOUFFLÉ

MAPLE MUSTARD-GLAZED CANADIAN BACON

CHAMPAGNE POACHED PEARS

No office to rush to, no place you have to be,

just the opportunity to sit back and enjoy a wonderful menu.

Relax, you have earned this time!

LADIES' *luncheon*

CHEDDAR WALNUT TOASTS

BROCCOLI SOUP

GRILLED CHICKEN BREASTS WITH BERRY SALSA

SAVORY GREEN BEANS

NUTTED RICE

LEMON COCONUT SQUARES

The South may no longer be about petticoats and
plantations, but Southern ladies still know how to pamper themselves.
Gather your closest girlfriends around and enjoy.

ITALIAN
interlude

TOMATO TART

HEARTS OF PALM SALAD

BAKED VEAL PARMESAN

BROCCOLI RISOTTO

SAUTÉED GREENS AND GARLIC

TIRAMISU

Nothing says romance like Italian food. Open up your
favorite bottle of wine and enjoy a menu to delight all the senses.

Bellissimo!

ELEGANT
evening

CRAB CAKES WITH SPICY RÉMOULADE

APPLE FETA SALAD

GRILLED LAMB CHOPS WITH ARTICHOKES AND OLIVES

PARMESAN POTATOES

LEMON PUDDING CAKE WITH BERRIES

As we try to simplify our lives, the need to embrace
elegance perseveres. Shine the silver and light the candles; a magnificent
table is all this menu needs to complete the magic.

MEXICAN
montage

LAYERED TACO DIP WITH TORTILLA CHIPS AND
CUMIN GUACAMOLE

BLACK BEAN PUMPKIN SOUP

SOUTHWESTERN SPOON BREAD

CHICKEN QUESADILLAS

RICE WITH ROASTED POBLANOS AND SPINACH

CLASSIC VANILLA FLAN

When the mood for fiesta hits, this Southwest menu will make

your guests sit up and say "OLÉ!"

SUMMER
social

SMOKED GOUDA AND CARAMELIZED ONION
QUESADILLAS

ASPARAGUS VINAIGRETTE

GOURMET MESCLUN WITH RASPBERRY VINAIGRETTE

BEEF KABOBS WITH HONEY GLAZE MARINADE

BALSAMIC ROASTED PORTOBELLO MUSHROOMS

ASIAN RICE PILAF

APRICOT BRANDY POUND CAKE

A casual gathering of friends on a warm summer

night is the perfect backdrop for this menu. Take advantage of all the

freshness the season has to offer.

DELECTABLE
dining

HOT PARMESAN ARTICHOKE DIP

MINI PRIME RIB TARTLETS

CRAB AND MUSHROOM CHEESECAKE

GREEK SALAD

BEEF TENDERLOIN WITH MAYTAG BLUE CHEESE SAUCE

SESAME ROASTED ASPARAGUS

ROASTED RED PEPPER POTATO CAKES

CARAMELIZED PEAR AND ALMOND TART

A casual gathering doesn't have to

mean burgers and fries. Invite your friends over and watch them

delight in this menu.

HOLIDAY
fare

SAVORY STUFFED ARTICHOKES

CRANBERRY MARMALADE BRIE

PINEAPPLE-GLAZED HAM

GREEN BEANS WITH CARAMELIZED ONIONS

CANDIED SWEET POTATOES

SOUTHERN PECAN PIE

This colorful menu is the perfect complement
to the festive holiday season. Enjoy this meal after you have trimmed
the tree and decked the halls.

NEW YEAR'S EVE
celebration

GRILLED QUAIL WITH HERBED CORN BREAD
AND BLACK CURRANT GLAZE

ENDIVE AND ARUGULA SALAD WITH
BURGUNDY POACHED PEARS

ORANGE CHAMPAGNE SORBET

FILLET OF BEEF IN PHYLLO PASTRY WITH
MADEIRA SAUCE

WILD MUSHROOM RISOTTO

RASPBERRY CRÈME BRÛLÉE

Old acquaintances may be forgot, but no

guest will ever forget this delicious menu. Make a resolution to accept

compliments graciously as the accolades fly.

Compliments of Priscilla Jackson, Executive Chef at B. McNeel's Restaurant.

COME ON IN...

appetizers and beverages

Like a fine wine, fine meals are best
enjoyed slowly and thoroughly.
Relax with the cocktail of your choice
in this beautiful setting.
We'll tantalize your taste buds with
an appetizer that hints
of the taste sensations to come.

ASIAN SPRING ROLLS

1 garlic clove, chopped
1/2 cup vegetable oil
2 pounds ground pork
1 pound fresh shrimp, chopped
4 cups cellophane noodles, soaked, drained
2 cups chopped bamboo shoots
1 cup dried black Chinese mushrooms, soaked, drained
1 cup chopped green onions
1 cup chopped fresh cilantro
5 tablespoons sugar
1 tablespoon fish sauce
1 teaspoon MSG (optional)
2 (16-ounce) packages egg roll wrappers
3 1/2 cups vegetable oil
2 to 3 eggs, beaten

Stir-fry the garlic in 1/2 cup oil in a wok or large skillet until light brown. Add the pork, shrimp, noodles, bamboo shoots, mushrooms, green onions, cilantro, sugar, fish sauce and MSG. Stir-fry until the pork is cooked through. Remove from the heat; cool.

For each egg roll, spoon about 1/4 cup of the pork mixture evenly down the center of an egg roll wrapper. Fold the ends over the filling and roll up in jelly roll fashion. Moisten the top edge with beaten egg and press firmly to seal.

Heat 3 1/2 cups oil to 365 degrees in a wok or large heavy saucepan. Deep-fry the egg rolls, a few at a time, until brown on all sides. Drain on paper towels. Serve with your favorite purchased sweet-and-sour sauce.

NOTE: Asian ingredients can be found at most large supermarkets or your local Asian market.

YIELD: 4 DOZEN EGG ROLLS

SAVORY STUFFED ARTICHOKES

2 cups fresh fine bread crumbs
3/4 cup grated Parmesan cheese
2 garlic cloves, minced
1/4 cup flat-leaf parsley, minced
Coarse salt and freshly ground pepper to taste
Juice of 1 lemon
6 medium artichokes
3/4 cup olive oil

Combine the bread crumbs and cheese in a medium bowl. Stir in the garlic and parsley. Season with salt and pepper; set aside.

Combine the lemon juice with enough cold water to cover the artichokes in a large bowl; set aside. Working quickly with 1 artichoke at a time, cut about 1/4 inch off the top with a sharp knife. Trim off the stem end to make a flat bottom. Snip off and discard the tip of each artichoke leaf with kitchen scissors. Rinse well under cold running water and immediately place in the lemon water. When all the artichokes have been prepared and soaked, remove them from the water. Shake them, upside down, to drain off the excess water. Place them upside down on a double thickness of paper towels to drain thoroughly.

Turn the drained artichokes over and season with salt and pepper. Stuff the bread crumb mixture generously between the leaves of each artichoke. Place the stuffed artichokes in a saucepan that will hold them tightly together. Drizzle 1/2 cup of the olive oil over the tops of the artichokes. Add enough water to the pan to come one-third of the way up the sides of the artichokes. Add the remaining 1/4 cup olive oil to the water in the pan. Bring to a boil, covered, over medium-high heat. Reduce the heat to low. Simmer for 1 1/2 hours or until the leaves can be easily pulled off. Remove the artichokes from the pan. Cool slightly before serving.

YIELD: 6 SERVINGS

MINI PRIME RIB TARTLETS

3 eggs, lightly beaten
1 cup flour
1 cup milk
1 (4- to 6-pound) prime rib roast
1 teaspoon salt
1 teaspoon pepper
Horseradish sauce
Sliced green onions

Combine the eggs, flour and milk in a bowl. Chill, covered, for 8 hours.

Sprinkle the roast with the salt and pepper. Place on a foil-lined rack in a roasting pan. Roast at 500 degrees for 30 minutes. Reduce the oven temperature to 350 degrees. Roast for 30 minutes. Increase the oven temperature to 450 degrees. Roast for 35 minutes or until the meat registers 140 to 160 degrees on a meat thermometer. Let stand, covered, for 15 minutes before carving into thin slices. Reserve 1/2 cup of the pan drippings.

Spoon the reserved pan drippings into miniature muffin cups, filling each 1/4 full. Heat at 450 degrees for 2 minutes or until hot. Stir the chilled batter. Spoon into the hot muffin cups, filling each 1/2 full. Bake at 450 degrees for 9 minutes or until the puddings are puffy and browned. Make a well in the center of each pudding. Arrange the meat slices in the wells. Remove from the muffin cups. Top with horseradish sauce and green onions. Serve warm.

YIELD: 64 TARTLETS

Signature Projects

The JLM was conceived in May of 1992 as a service vehicle for Rutherford County women and children. This vision has resulted in eight major community service projects that the JLM considers its "signature projects." The groundwork laid by "first president" Anne Davis and her successor Alicia Hollis established this group as a full-fledged Junior League in record time. Through the strong leadership and hard work of JLM members, the tradition of reaching out in service to the community continues today.

COME ON IN...

CRAB CAKES WITH SPICY RÉMOULADE

1 pound jumbo lump crab meat, flaked
1 egg, beaten
1/2 cup mayonnaise
1/2 cup each chopped red onion and red bell pepper
1 tablespoon Dijon mustard
1/2 cup chopped fresh parsley
Juice of 2 lemons
1 teaspoon each cayenne pepper and paprika
Tabasco sauce to taste
Salt to taste
1 3/4 cups fine bread crumbs
1/4 cup vegetable oil
2 tablespoons unsalted butter
Spicy Rémoulade (below)

Combine the crab meat, egg, mayonnaise, onion, bell pepper, Dijon mustard and parsley in a bowl. Add the next 5 ingredients. Toss to combine. Add enough of the bread crumbs to make the mixture firm but still moist. Form into 12 small patties. Coat the crab cakes in the remaining bread crumbs. Heat the oil in a nonstick ovenproof sauté pan over medium heat. Add the crab cakes. Sauté for 2 minutes or until lightly browned on 1 side. Add the butter to the pan and turn the crab cakes over. Bake at 400 degrees for 8 minutes or until the crab cakes are browned. Drain on paper towels. Serve warm with Spicy Rémoulade.

YIELD: 6 TO 8 SERVINGS

SPICY RÉMOULADE

1 cup mayonnaise
3 tablespoons each chopped fresh parsley and minced capers
1 tablespoon Thai chile paste
1 1/2 teaspoons horseradish
Salt and pepper to taste

Combine the ingredients in a small bowl. Chill, covered, for up to 3 days.

NOTE: Thai chile paste is available at Asian markets.

YIELD: ABOUT 1 CUP

SMOKED GOUDA AND CARAMELIZED ONION QUESADILLAS

Add sliced grilled chicken to make this an entrée.

> *2 tablespoons butter*
> *1 onion, thinly sliced*
> *1 tablespoon brown sugar*
> *¹/4 teaspoon balsamic vinegar*
> *1¹/2 cups shredded smoked Gouda cheese*
> *4 (10-inch) flour tortillas*
> *6 slices bacon, crisp-cooked, crumbled, or 2 ounces prosciutto, chopped*
> *Pepper to taste*
> *2 tablespoons butter, melted*

Melt 2 tablespoons butter in a heavy medium skillet over medium heat. Add the onion, brown sugar and vinegar. Sauté for 25 minutes or until the onion is lightly browned, stirring frequently. Remove from the heat. Cool to room temperature.

Sprinkle the cheese over half of each tortilla, dividing it equally. Top with the bacon and onion mixture. Season with pepper. Fold the other half of each tortilla over the filling. Brush the tortillas with some of the melted butter.

Brush a large heavy skillet with some of the remaining melted butter. Heat over medium-high heat. Add the quesadillas, in batches, to the skillet. Cook for 2 minutes on each side or just until brown spots appear, brushing the skillet with butter between batches. Transfer the quesadillas to a large baking sheet.

Bake at 350 degrees for 5 minutes or until lightly browned and the cheese melts. Cut each quesadilla into 6 wedges. Arrange on a serving platter and serve hot.

YIELD: 6 SERVINGS

CHICKEN QUESADILLAS

1 1/2 to 2 pounds boneless skinless chicken, cut into strips
2 tablespoons olive oil
1 garlic clove, minced
1 green bell pepper, chopped
1 (12-ounce) bottle salsa
6 (6-inch) flour tortillas
2 cups shredded Monterey Jack cheese

Sauté the chicken in the olive oil in a skillet. Add the garlic and bell pepper. Cook for 5 minutes or until the chicken is no longer pink. Stir in the salsa. Cook until heated through.

Layer the tortillas, chicken mixture and cheese 1/2 at a time in a greased 9×13-inch baking dish. Bake, covered, at 350 degrees for 30 minutes.

YIELD: 8 SERVINGS

SPINACH AND FETA CROSTINI

1 (10-ounce) package frozen chopped spinach, thawed, well drained
2 plum tomatoes, coarsely chopped
1 small onion, coarsely chopped
1/2 cup crumbled feta cheese
1/4 cup each mayonnaise and sour cream
1 garlic clove, minced
1/4 teaspoon pepper
1 (16-ounce) loaf French bread, cut into 1/2-inch slices

Combine the first 8 ingredients in a bowl. Spread on 1 side of each bread slice. Arrange the bread slices on a baking sheet. Bake at 350 degrees for 18 minutes or until lightly browned.

NOTE: Garlic clove skins can be removed easily if the clove is warmed in the microwave for about 15 seconds.

YIELD: 24 SERVINGS

BIG WHEEL SANDWICH BITES

1 (16-ounce) loaf Hawaiian bread
Ranch salad dressing
Turkey slices
American or Cheddar cheese slices
Ham slices
Swiss cheese slices
3 slices bacon, crisp-cooked
3 tablespoons butter, melted
Poppy seeds
Lettuce

Freeze the bread for 15 minutes or until firm. Cut the loaf horizontally into fourths. Spread the bottom bread layer with ranch dressing and top with turkey and American cheese. Cover with the next bread layer. Spread with dressing and top with ham, Swiss cheese and the next bread layer. Spread with dressing and top with the bacon and top bread layer. Brush the melted butter over the sandwich and sprinkle with poppy seeds.

Wrap the sandwich in foil. Bake at 350 degrees for 20 to 25 minutes. Unwrap the sandwich and add the lettuce. Cut into small pieces to serve.

NOTE: May also cut the sandwich into wedges like a pie to serve as a main dish.

YIELD: 12 SERVINGS

BRIE AND ARTICHOKE FOCACCIA

1 (10-inch) square or round focaccia, about 2 inches thick, split into halves horizontally
1 (8-ounce) wheel Brie cheese, rind removed, cut into large chunks
1 (14-ounce) can artichoke hearts, drained, chopped
4 slices bacon, crisp-cooked, crumbled

Toast the focaccia, cut sides up, just until crisp; set aside. Place the cheese in a medium microwave-safe bowl. Microwave on High for 30 to 45 seconds or until the cheese begins to melt. Stir in the artichokes and bacon. Microwave for 1 to 1^1/$_2$ minutes or until heated through, stirring once or twice. Spread the cheese mixture over the focaccia bottom. Cover with the focaccia top and place on a baking sheet. Bake at 400 degrees for 8 to 10 minutes or until heated through. Cut into 1×4-inch strips or wedges. Garnish with fresh rosemary.

NOTE: May substitute a Boboli pizza crust for the focaccia. Spread the cheese mixture evenly over the crust. Serve open face, sprinkling fresh rosemary over the cheese on each half.

YIELD: 12 SERVINGS

CHEDDAR WALNUT TOASTS

8 (6-inch) whole wheat pita breads, split horizontally
12 ounces sharp Cheddar cheese, shredded
1/4 cup (1/2 stick) unsalted butter, softened
1/4 cup dry sherry
1/2 teaspoon salt
Tabasco sauce to taste
1 1/2 cups walnuts, lightly toasted, finely chopped

Cut each pita bread into 4 wedges. Toast until crisp; set aside.

Beat the cheese, butter, sherry, salt and Tabasco sauce in a mixing bowl until well blended. Stir in the walnuts. Spread the cheese mixture over the toasted pita wedges. Arrange the pita on a baking sheet.

Broil for 1 to 2 minutes or until the cheese topping is lightly browned and bubbly.

YIELD: 64 TOASTS

CHEESE STRAWS

1/2 cup (1 stick) butter or margarine, softened
8 ounces sharp Cheddar cheese, shredded
1/2 teaspoon salt
1/2 teaspoon cayenne pepper
1 1/2 cups flour, sifted

Combine the butter, cheese, salt and cayenne pepper in a bowl and blend well. Add the flour gradually, stirring to form a dough. Place the dough in a cookie press fitted with a star tip. Press onto a greased baking sheet into long strips. Cut the strips at 4-inch intervals to form cheese straws. (Or roll the dough 1/4 inch thick and score the surface with a fork. Cut the dough into strips.) Bake at 350 degrees for 20 to 25 minutes.

NOTE: May also roll the dough into 1/2-inch balls. Press the dough balls into circles and score them with a fork.

YIELD: 5 DOZEN

HOT PARMESAN ARTICHOKE DIP

8 ounces cream cheese, softened
1 1/2 cups sour cream
1 cup shredded Parmesan cheese
1/4 cup mayonnaise
2 teaspoons (or more) dillweed
1 (14-ounce) can artichoke hearts, drained, finely chopped
1 tablespoon shredded Parmesan cheese

Beat the cream cheese, sour cream, 1 cup Parmesan cheese, mayonnaise and dillweed in a mixing bowl until smooth. Fold in the artichokes. Spoon into a shallow baking dish. Top with 1 tablespoon Parmesan cheese. Bake at 350 degrees for 40 minutes. Serve warm with crackers, toasted baguette slices, tortilla chips or fresh vegetables.

NOTE: May prepare this dip up to 2 days ahead of time. Chill, covered, then bring to room temperature before baking.

YIELD: ABOUT 4 CUPS

MARINATED BLACK-EYED PEA DIP

2 (15-ounce) cans black-eyed peas, drained
1/2 cup finely chopped yellow or red bell pepper
1/2 cup finely chopped red onion
1/2 garlic clove, minced
1/4 cup each balsamic vinegar and extra-virgin olive oil
3 tablespoons sugar
1/2 teaspoon salt

Combine the black-eyed peas, bell pepper, onion, garlic, vinegar, olive oil, sugar and salt in a bowl. Chill, covered, for 24 hours, stirring 2 to 3 times. Serve with corn chips, toasted croutons or wheat crackers.

YIELD: ABOUT 4 CUPS

SMOKY MOUNTAIN BEEF DIP

1 pound ground beef
3/4 cup chopped onion
1/2 cup chopped red bell pepper
1/2 garlic clove, minced
1 (8-ounce) can tomato sauce
1/4 cup ketchup
1 teaspoon each sugar and salt
3/4 teaspoon oregano
1/4 teaspoon pepper
8 ounces cream cheese, cubed
1/3 cup grated Parmesan cheese

Brown the ground beef with the onion, bell pepper and garlic in a skillet, stirring until the ground beef is crumbly and the onion is tender; drain. Stir in the tomato sauce, ketchup, sugar, salt, oregano and pepper. Simmer gently, covered, for 10 minutes. Add the cream cheese and Parmesan cheese. Heat until the cream cheese melts and the mixture is well blended, stirring constantly. Serve warm with dip-size corn chips.

YIELD: 12 SERVINGS

FRESH VEGETABLE DIP

Serve this dip in a red, green, or yellow bell pepper that has been hollowed out for a colorful alternative to a bowl.

1/3 cup shredded carrot
1/4 cup shredded cabbage
2 tablespoons finely chopped green bell pepper
1 tablespoon finely chopped onion
1 cup sour cream
2 tablespoons mayonnaise
1 teaspoon tarragon vinegar
3/4 teaspoon garlic salt

Combine the carrot, cabbage, bell pepper and onion in a bowl. Stir in the sour cream, mayonnaise, vinegar and garlic salt. Chill, covered, in the refrigerator. Serve with fresh vegetables.

YIELD: 8 TO 10 SERVINGS

CUMIN GUACAMOLE

2 ripe avocados
1/2 cup sour cream
1 tomato, coarsely chopped
2 green onions, chopped
1 teaspoon cumin
1 tablespoon lemon juice
Salt to taste
Pepper to taste

Mash the avocados in a bowl. Add the sour cream, tomato, green onions, cumin and lemon juice and mix well. Season to taste with salt and pepper. Serve with tortilla chips.

YIELD: ABOUT 2 1/2 CUPS

LAYERED TACO DIP

1 (16-ounce) can refried beans
1 envelope taco seasoning mix
Tabasco sauce to taste
3/4 cup sour cream
1 medium onion, chopped
1 (2-ounce) can sliced black olives, drained
8 ounces Monterey Jack cheese with jalapeño chiles, shredded
3 plum tomatoes, seeded, chopped
Pickled jalapeño chiles (optional)

Combine the beans, Tabasco sauce and taco seasoning mix in a bowl, blending well. Spread over the bottom of a 12-inch pan. Layer the sour cream, onion, olives, cheese and tomatoes over the bean mixture. Top with pickled jalapeño chiles.

NOTE: Low-fat and fat-free ingredients do not affect the taste of this dip.

YIELD: 12 SERVINGS

CORN AND BLACK BEAN DIP

1 (15-ounce) can black beans, rinsed, drained
1 (11-ounce) can yellow and white corn, drained
2 large tomatoes, coarsely chopped, or 1 pint cherry tomatoes, quartered
1 medium avocado, coarsely chopped
6 green onions, finely chopped
1/2 cup vegetable oil
1/4 cup red wine vinegar
1/4 teaspoon salt
1/4 to 1/2 teaspoon cayenne pepper

Combine the beans, corn, tomatoes, avocado, green onions, oil, vinegar, salt and cayenne pepper in a bowl. Chill for 8 to 10 hours. Taste and adjust the seasonings before serving.

YIELD: ABOUT 5 CUPS

STUFFED TOMATOES WITH SPINACH AND RICOTTA

1 medium yellow onion, finely chopped
1 tablespoon extra-virgin olive oil
1 (10-ounce) package frozen chopped spinach, thawed, squeezed dry
Salt and pepper to taste
1/8 teaspoon nutmeg
8 ounces ricotta cheese
2 egg yolks
1/2 cup pine nuts
1/2 cup chopped flat-leaf parsley
1/4 cup freshly grated Parmesan cheese
48 Cherry Tomato Cups (below)
Additional Parmesan cheese

Cook the onion in the olive oil in a covered skillet over low heat for 15 minutes or until tender and lightly browned. Stir in the spinach. Season with salt, pepper and nutmeg. Cook, covered, for 10 minutes, stirring frequently.

Beat the ricotta cheese and egg yolks in a mixing bowl until thoroughly combined. Add the spinach mixture, pine nuts, parsley and 1/4 cup Parmesan cheese and mix well. Season with salt and pepper.

Blot the Cherry Tomato Cups with paper towels to remove any excess moisture. Spoon the spinach mixture into the tomato cups. Place in a baking dish. Sprinkle additional Parmesan cheese over the top of the cups. Bake at 350 degrees for 10 minutes or until hot and bubbly.

YIELD: 4 DOZEN

CHERRY TOMATO CUPS: For each cup, remove the top of a cherry tomato. Scoop out and discard the seeds and flesh, taking care not to pierce the side of the tomato. Sprinkle the inside of the tomato lightly with salt. Place upside down on paper towels for 30 minutes to drain.

BASIL CHEESE TORTA

8 ounces cream cheese, softened
4 ounces feta cheese
2 tablespoons butter, softened
1 cup prepared pesto
12 ounces provolone cheese slices
2 cups roasted red pepper salsa
1/4 cup chopped pine nuts, toasted

Combine the cream cheese, feta cheese and butter in a blender or food processor and process until smooth, stopping to scrape down the side of the container. Add the pesto and process until well blended; set aside.

Line a 4×8-inch loaf pan with plastic wrap, letting 1 inch of the wrap extend over each side. Arrange 1/3 of the provolone cheese slices on the bottom and up the sides of the pan. Layer 1/2 of the pesto mixture, 1/3 cup salsa and 2 tablespoons pine nuts over the cheese. Top with 1/2 of the remaining cheese slices. Continue layering with the remaining pesto mixture, 1/3 cup salsa, remaining pine nuts and cheese slices, gently pressing each layer. Fold the outer cheese slices toward the center. Chill, covered, for 8 hours.

Uncover the torta and invert onto a serving platter. Top with 1/3 cup salsa. Garnish with fresh basil leaves and pine nuts. Serve with remaining 1 cup salsa and toasted French baguette slices.

YIELD: 12 SERVINGS

TUSCAN TERRINE

8 ounces cream cheese, softened
8 ounces goat cheese, softened
$1/2$ cup sun-dried tomato purée
$1/3$ cup prepared pesto
2 tablespoons roasted garlic purée
Salt and pepper to taste

Beat the cream cheese and goat cheese in a medium mixing bowl until smooth. Divide the cheese mixture evenly among 3 bowls. Add the tomato purée, pesto and garlic each to a separate bowl of the cheese mixture and mix each one well. Season each cheese mixture with salt and pepper.

Line a 3-cup straight-sided mold with dampened cheesecloth, draping any excess over the edge of the mold. Layer the pesto, garlic cheese mixture and tomato mixture in the mold, smoothing each layer with a rubber spatula. Fold the excess cheesecloth over the top. Chill for 1 hour.

To serve, unfold the cheesecloth and invert the terrine onto a serving platter. Remove the mold and cheesecloth. Serve with crackers.

NOTE: The sun-dried tomato purée, pesto and roasted garlic purée are available at most supermarkets.

YIELD: 3 CUPS

CRAB AND MUSHROOM CHEESECAKE

CRUST
1 cup fresh French bread crumbs
1 cup freshly grated Parmesan cheese
6 tablespoons butter, melted

FILLING
1 tablespoon olive oil
1 cup chopped onion
1 cup chopped red bell pepper
4 cups coarsely chopped assorted wild mushrooms (cremini, oyster, shiitake)
1 ounce dried wild mushrooms, soaked, drained, chopped
28 ounces cream cheese, softened
2 teaspoons salt
1 teaspoon pepper
4 eggs
1/2 cup heavy cream
10 ounces canned crab meat, drained, flaked
1 cup shredded smoked Gouda cheese
1/2 cup chopped fresh parsley

For the crust, combine the bread crumbs, Parmesan cheese and butter in a bowl until well blended. Press onto the bottom of a 9- or 10-inch springform pan. Bake at 325 degrees for 15 minutes or until lightly browned. Cool on a wire rack.

For the filling, heat the olive oil in a large heavy skillet over medium-high heat. Add the onion and bell pepper. Sauté for 2 minutes. Add the mushrooms. Sauté for 10 minutes or until the liquid evaporates and the mushrooms begin to brown. Remove from the heat; cool.

Beat the cream cheese, salt and pepper in a large mixing bowl until fluffy. Add the eggs 1 at a time, beating well after each addition. Beat in the heavy cream. Stir in the onion mixture, crab meat, Gouda cheese and parsley. Pour over the crust. Place the filled springform pan on a baking sheet. Bake at 325 degrees for 1 1/2 hours or until the top is puffed and browned and the center moves slightly when the pan is shaken. Cool on a wire rack. Serve warm or chilled. Store, covered, in the refrigerator.

YIELD: 20 SERVINGS

CRANBERRY MARMALADE BRIE

12 ounces fresh cranberries
3/4 cup packed light brown sugar
1/3 cup currants
1/3 cup water
1/4 teaspoon dry mustard
1/4 teaspoon ginger
1/4 teaspoon allspice
1/4 teaspoon ground cloves
1 (8-inch) wheel Brie cheese

Combine the cranberries, brown sugar, currants, water, dry mustard, ginger, allspice and cloves in a heavy nonaluminum saucepan. Cook over medium-high heat for 5 minutes or until the cranberries burst, stirring frequently. Remove from the heat and cool to room temperature. Refrigerate, covered, until chilled. (May be stored up to 3 days at this point.)

Cut out a circle in the top rind of the Brie cheese, leaving a 1/2-inch border of the rind intact. Discard the circle of rind. Place the Brie on a foil-lined baking sheet. Spread the cranberry marmalade over the top of the Brie. Chill, covered, for up to 6 hours.

Uncover the Brie. Bake at 300 degrees for 12 minutes or until the cheese is soft. Do not overbake. Serve on a platter surrounded by assorted crackers and fruit, such as apple and orange slices.

YIELD: 10 SERVINGS

KAHLÚA BRIE

1 (8-ounce) wheel Brie cheese, rind removed
3/4 cup chopped pecans
1/4 cup Kahlúa
3 tablespoons brown sugar

Place the Brie cheese in a small baking dish. Combine the pecans, Kahlúa and brown sugar in a bowl. Spread over the top of the Brie. Bake at 350 degrees for 15 minutes or until soft. (Be careful not to overbake.) Serve warm with crackers.

YIELD: 10 TO 12 SERVINGS

HOMEMADE HERB BOURSIN CHEESE

8 ounces cream cheese, softened
1/2 cup (1 stick) butter, softened
1/4 teaspoon minced garlic
1/8 teaspoon marjoram
1/8 teaspoon thyme
1/8 teaspoon oregano
1/8 teaspoon basil
1/8 teaspoon pepper

Blend the cream cheese, butter, garlic, marjoram, thyme, oregano, basil and pepper in a bowl until smooth. Chill, covered, for several hours. Serve with crackers or as a spread for sandwiches and wraps.

YIELD: 1 1/2 CUPS

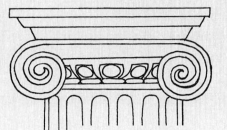

OLIVE SPREAD TEA SANDWICHES

8 ounces cream cheese, softened
1/3 cup chopped pimento-stuffed olives
2 tablespoons olive juice
1/4 cup finely chopped pecans
8 slices bacon, crisp-cooked, crumbled
Thinly sliced sandwich bread, crusts removed

Combine the cream cheese, olives, olive juice, pecans and bacon in a small bowl and mix until well blended. Spread on the sandwich bread slices to make mini sandwiches. Cut into triangles or other shapes. Garnish with an olive slice.

NOTE: May also use as a spread for crackers.

YIELD: 8 SERVINGS

Baby Love

In coordination with the Health Department, the JLM has encouraged immunizations of infants throughout Rutherford County. Through a gift certificate incentive program, JLM members encourage and remind new mothers to immunize their babies. Since the inception of this program in 1991, thousands of babies have been given a healthy start to their first year of life.

CITRUS FRUIT SPREAD

16 ounces cream cheese, softened
1/4 cup (1/2 stick) butter, softened
1 cup sifted confectioners' sugar
2 tablespoons orange juice
1 tablespoon grated orange zest
1/2 teaspoon vanilla extract
1 cup finely chopped walnuts or pecans
Grated zest of 1 orange

Beat the cream cheese, butter, confectioners' sugar, orange juice, 1 tablespoon orange zest and vanilla in a bowl until smooth. Chill, covered, for at least 30 minutes.

Divide the chilled cheese mixture in half. Shape each half into a ball. Roll in the walnuts and orange zest to coat. Chill for 30 minutes before serving. Serve with apples, pears, strawberries, muffins and gingersnaps.

YIELD: 16 SERVINGS

SPICED PECANS

1 egg white
1 tablespoon water
1 pound pecan halves
2/3 cup sugar
1 teaspoon cinnamon
1/4 teaspoon salt

Beat the egg white and water in a large bowl with a fork until foamy. Add the pecans and stir to coat. Combine the sugar, cinnamon and salt in a bowl. Pour over the pecans and mix until coated. Spread the pecans in a 10×15-inch baking pan.

Bake at 300 degrees for 15 minutes. Stir the pecans, scraping the bottom of the pan. Continue baking for 15 minutes, stirring again after 10 minutes. Pour the pecans immediately into a bowl to prevent them from sticking to the pan.

YIELD: 4 CUPS

ALMOND TEA

Fabulous brunch tea!

3 lemons
1 quart water
2 cups sugar
1 teaspoon vanilla extract
1 teaspoon almond extract
2¹/₂ cups pineapple juice
2 cups very strong brewed tea
1 (1-liter) bottle ginger ale

Squeeze the lemons, reserving the juice and rinds. Combine the lemon rinds, water and sugar in a saucepan. Bring to a boil; remove from the heat. Remove and discard the rinds. Stir in the reserved lemon juice, vanilla, almond extract, pineapple juice and tea. Freeze the tea mixture in a container that will fit inside a punch bowl.

When ready to serve, thaw the frozen tea mixture just until it can be removed from its container. Place in a punch bowl. Pour the ginger ale over the top. Let stand for 10 to 15 minutes before serving.

YIELD: 8 SERVINGS

CAPPUCCINO BLAST

4 cups water
4 cups sugar
1/4 cup instant coffee granules (regular or decaffeinated)
1/2 gallon vanilla ice cream, softened
1/2 gallon chocolate ice cream, softened
2 quarts milk

Bring the water to a boil in a saucepan. Stir in the sugar and coffee granules. Cook until the sugar and coffee are dissolved. Pour 1 1/2 cups of the coffee mixture into a large bowl or punch bowl. (Freeze the remaining coffee mixture for later use.) Add the vanilla ice cream, chocolate ice cream and milk. Stir until the ice cream is the desired consistency. Garnish with chocolate shavings and cinnamon.

YIELD: 12 TO 16 SERVINGS

SANGRIA BLANCA

1 cup water
1/2 cup sugar
2 (750-milliliter) bottles chablis
1/2 cup Triple Sec
1 lemon, sliced
2 limes, sliced
2 oranges, sliced
2 cups sparkling mineral water, chilled

Combine the water and sugar in a small saucepan. Bring to a boil over medium heat. Simmer for 5 minutes or until the sugar is dissolved. Remove from the heat and cool to room temperature. Combine the sugar syrup, chablis, Triple Sec, lemon, limes and oranges in a pitcher or bowl. Refrigerate, covered, until chilled.

Just before serving, pour the wine mixture into a larger pitcher or punch bowl. Stir in the sparkling water. Serve over ice. Garnish each glass with additional citrus slices, strawberries and/or kiwifruit slices.

YIELD: 12 SERVINGS

WINTER FRUIT SANGRIA

2 (750-milliliter) bottles fruity white wine
8 ounces seedless green grapes, halved
2 Red Delicious apples, thinly sliced
2 cups apple juice
1 cup pineapple juice

Combine the wine, grapes and apples in a pitcher. Let stand for at least 1 hour. Stir in the apple juice and pineapple juice. Serve over ice.

YIELD: 16 TO 20 SERVINGS

RUM PUNCH

³/4 cup light rum
¹/2 cup gin
¹/2 cup fruit juice
¹/2 cup pineapple juice
¹/2 cup lemon juice

Combine the rum, gin, fruit juice, pineapple juice and lemon juice in a pitcher. Pour into rock glasses. Garnish with maraschino cherries and orange slices.

YIELD: 4 SERVINGS

HOLIDAY EGGNOG

4 ounces each bourbon, brandy and Tia Maria
12 egg yolks
1/2 pound confectioners' sugar
1 quart each whipping cream and half-and-half
12 egg whites

Combine the bourbon, brandy, Tia Maria and egg yolks in a bowl. Add the confectioners' sugar. Beat until thoroughly mixed. Chill, covered, for at least 24 hours. Beat the whipping cream in a mixing bowl until thick but not stiff. Stir in the half-and-half and chilled egg yolk mixture. Beat the egg whites in a mixing bowl until soft peaks form. Fold into the cream mixture. Serve with nutmeg sprinkled over the top.

NOTE: To avoid raw eggs that may carry salmonella, we suggest using an equivalent amount of pasteurized egg substitute.

YIELD: 16 SERVINGS

WASSAIL

6 cinnamon sticks
16 whole cloves
1 teaspoon ground allspice
2 cups cranberry juice
6 cups apple juice
1/4 cup sugar
1 teaspoon bitters
1/4 cup rum (optional)

Tie the cinnamon sticks, cloves and allspice in a cheesecloth bag. Combine the spice bag, cranberry juice, apple juice, sugar and bitters in a saucepan. Bring to a boil. Reduce the heat to low. Simmer for 10 minutes. Remove and discard the spice bag. Stir in the rum. Serve hot.

NOTE: To make this for a large group, use a 30-cup electric percolator. Place the same amounts of spices as listed above into the coffee basket. Use four times the juices, sugar and bitters.

YIELD: 8 SERVINGS

KITCHEN TABLE TREATS

soups and salads

Looking out the windows, we can see
another beautiful day in Middle Tennessee.
A steaming bowl of soup and a
fresh salad will warm up your appetite
for the party that is just beginning.

BLACK BEAN PUMPKIN SOUP

3 (15-ounce) cans black beans, rinsed, drained
1 cup drained canned tomatoes, chopped
$1/4$ cup ($1/2$ stick) unsalted butter
$1^{1}/4$ cups chopped onions
$1/2$ cup minced shallots
4 garlic cloves, minced
1 tablespoon plus 2 teaspoons cumin
1 teaspoon salt
$1/2$ teaspoon freshly ground pepper
4 cups beef broth
1 (15-ounce) can pumpkin
$1/2$ cup dry sherry
$1/2$ pound ham, diced
3 to 4 tablespoons sherry vinegar

Combine 2 cans of the beans and the tomatoes in a food processor and process until coarsely puréed; set aside.

Melt the butter in a heavy, 6-quart pot over medium heat. Add the onions, shallots, garlic, cumin, salt and pepper. Cook until the onions are tender and starting to brown, stirring constantly. Stir in the puréed bean mixture, the remaining 1 can whole beans, broth, pumpkin and sherry. Bring to a boil. Reduce the heat to low. Simmer for 25 minutes or until the soup is thick enough to coat the back of a spoon, stirring occasionally. (May be prepared in advance to this point and chilled.)

Just before serving, stir in the ham and vinegar. Simmer until heated through, stirring frequently. Season with salt and pepper. Serve garnished with sour cream and toasted pumpkin seeds.

NOTE: May substitute shrimp, chicken or sausage for the ham.

YIELD: 6 SERVINGS

BROCCOLI SOUP

This soup is wonderful on cold winter nights. Serve with French bread and salad for a quick weekday meal.

3/4 cup finely chopped onion
2 tablespoons vegetable oil
6 cups water
6 chicken bouillon cubes
8 ounces fine egg noodles
Salt to taste
2 (10-ounce) packages frozen chopped broccoli
1/8 teaspoon garlic powder
6 cups milk
1 pound Velveeta cheese, cubed
Pepper to taste

Sauté the onion in the oil in a saucepan until tender. Add the water and bouillon cubes. Bring to a boil. Add the noodles and salt. Cook for 8 to 10 minutes or until the noodles are tender. Add the broccoli and garlic powder. Return to a boil. Cook until the broccoli is tender. Add the milk, Velveeta and pepper. Cook over medium heat until the Velveeta melts, stirring occasionally.

YIELD: 4 TO 6 SERVINGS

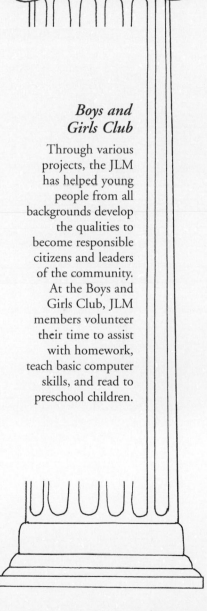

Boys and Girls Club

Through various projects, the JLM has helped young people from all backgrounds develop the qualities to become responsible citizens and leaders of the community. At the Boys and Girls Club, JLM members volunteer their time to assist with homework, teach basic computer skills, and read to preschool children.

FIESTA CHILI

This chili is more full flavored if made a day ahead.

> 5 medium yellow onions, chopped
> 3 garlic cloves, chopped or minced
> 3 tablespoons extra-virgin olive oil
> 3 pounds ground beef, browned, drained
> 2 (28-ounce) cans whole tomatoes, chopped
> 1 cup dry red wine
> ^{1}/$_4$ cup plus 2 tablespoons chili powder
> 2 teaspoons oregano
> ^{1}/$_2$ teaspoon Tabasco sauce
> Salt and pepper to taste
> ^{1}/$_2$ cup sour cream
> ^{1}/$_2$ cup pitted black olives, chopped
> ^{1}/$_2$ cup pine nuts, toasted (optional)

Sauté the onions and garlic in the olive oil in a pot until tender but not browned. Stir in the browned ground beef, undrained tomatoes, wine, chili powder, oregano, Tabasco sauce, salt and pepper. Cook over medium heat for 1 hour, stirring occasionally. Taste and adjust the seasonings. Serve individual portions topped with sour cream, olives and pine nuts.

To prevent tears when peeling and chopping onions, chill the onion in the refrigerator first.

NOTE: May add 2 (15-ounce) cans red beans, rinsed and drained, with the ground beef to bulk up the chili.

YIELD: 8 SERVINGS

STONE CRAB BISQUE

1/2 cup (1 stick) butter or margarine
1/2 cup finely chopped onion
1/2 cup finely chopped red bell pepper
2 green onions, finely chopped
1/4 cup chopped fresh parsley
8 ounces fresh mushrooms, chopped
1/4 cup flour
2 cups milk
2 teaspoons salt
3 cups half-and-half
1 teaspoon hot red pepper sauce
1/4 teaspoon black pepper
2 1/2 cups stone crab claw meat
1/4 cup dry sherry

Melt 1/4 cup of the butter in a Dutch oven over medium-high heat. Add the onion, bell pepper, green onions, parsley and mushrooms. Cook for 5 minutes or until tender, stirring constantly. Remove from the pan; set aside.

Melt the remaining 1/4 cup butter in the same pan over low heat. Add the flour, stirring until smooth. Cook for 1 minute, stirring constantly. Stir in the milk gradually. Cook over medium heat until thickened and bubbly, stirring constantly. Stir in the onion mixture, salt, half-and-half, pepper sauce and black pepper. Bring to a boil, stirring constantly. Reduce the heat to low. Stir in the crab meat gently. Simmer for 5 minutes, stirring frequently. Stir in the sherry and serve.

YIELD: 8 SERVINGS

BAKED POTATO SOUP

4 large baking potatoes
2/3 cup butter or margarine
2/3 cup flour
6 cups milk
3/4 teaspoon salt
1/2 teaspoon pepper
4 green onions, chopped
12 slices bacon, crisp-cooked, crumbled
1 1/4 cups shredded Cheddar cheese
1 cup sour cream

Scrub the potatoes and prick each in several places with a fork. Bake at 400 degrees for 1 hour or until tender. Cool completely. Cut the potatoes lengthwise into halves. Scoop out the pulp and set aside. Discard the skins.

Melt the butter in a saucepan over low heat. Add the flour, stirring until smooth. Cook for 1 minute, stirring constantly. Stir in the milk gradually. Cook over medium heat until thickened and bubbly, stirring constantly. Add the potato pulp, salt, pepper, 2 tablespoons of the green onions, 1/2 cup of the bacon and 1 cup of the cheese. Cook until heated through. Stir in the sour cream. Heat gently but do not boil. Stir in additional milk, if necessary, to achieve the desired consistency. Serve topped with the remaining green onions, bacon and 1/4 cup cheese.

YIELD: 8 SERVINGS

TORTELLINI SOUP

3 (14-ounce) cans chicken broth
2 (9-ounce) packages refrigerated cheese tortellini
1 (14-ounce) can diced Italian-style tomatoes
4 green onions, chopped
2 garlic cloves, minced
2 teaspoons minced fresh basil, or 1 teaspoon dried basil

Bring the broth to a boil in a large saucepan over medium-high heat. Add the tortellini, undrained tomatoes, green onions, garlic and basil. Return to a boil. Reduce the heat to low. Simmer for 10 minutes. Garnish with shredded Parmesan cheese.

NOTE: Two tablespoons vermouth is a wonderful addition to this soup.

YIELD: 6 SERVINGS

APPLE FETA SALAD

1 head romaine, torn into pieces
2 apples, cut into chunks
3 ribs celery, cut into pieces
Feta cheese
$1/2$ cup walnuts, toasted, coarsely chopped
$1/4$ cup raisins
3 tablespoons olive oil
1 tablespoon cider vinegar
Salt and freshly ground pepper to taste

Combine the romaine, apples, celery, cheese, walnuts and raisins in a salad bowl. Whisk the olive oil, vinegar, salt and pepper in a small bowl until combined. Toss enough of the dressing with the salad to lightly coat. Serve immediately.

NOTE: May substitute toasted pecans for the walnuts.

YIELD: 6 SERVINGS

MIXED GREENS WITH BLEU CHEESE AND AVOCADO

1 head romaine, torn into pieces
1 small head endive, torn into pieces
1 head radicchio, torn into pieces
1/2 cup crumbled bleu cheese
1 ripe avocado, halved
2 tablespoons pine nuts, toasted
1 tablespoon minced red onion
1/4 cup balsamic vinegar
2 to 3 tablespoons mayonnaise
1 tablespoon horseradish, or to taste
1 tablespoon Dijon mustard, or to taste
1/4 cup extra-virgin olive oil
Salt and pepper to taste
Croutons

Toss the romaine, endive and radicchio in a large bowl. Add the cheese, spoonfuls of the avocado, pine nuts and onion. Toss to combine.

Combine the vinegar, mayonnaise, horseradish and Dijon mustard in a small bowl. Whisk in the olive oil. Taste and adjust the seasonings. Add the dressing to the salad. Toss until the avocado and cheese are well coated. Season with salt and pepper. Top with croutons.

NOTE: To perk up leafy greens, separate the stalks and make a fresh cut on the bottom. Place in a bowl of ice cold water for a few hours. To dry the greens after rinsing, place in a plastic bag with paper towels and spin around a few times.

YIELD: 6 TO 8 SERVINGS

ENDIVE AND ARUGULA SALAD WITH BURGUNDY POACHED PEARS

PEARS
3 cups port wine
1 1/2 cups sugar
Juice of 1 lemon
2 tablespoons orange zest
1 vanilla bean
1 cinnamon stick
8 Anjou pears, peeled

PORT WINE VINAIGRETTE
1 1/2 cups poaching liquid
2 cups vegetable oil
Salt and pepper to taste

SALAD
4 heads endive, torn into pieces
8 ounces arugula
2 cups crumbled Gorgonzola cheese

For the pears, combine the port, sugar, lemon juice, orange zest, vanilla bean and cinnamon stick in a saucepan. Add the pears. Bring to a simmer. Cook for 20 minutes or until the pears are tender. Remove from the heat. Place the pan in a bowl of ice water to cool. Chill the pears in the poaching liquid until cold. Remove the pears from the poaching liquid, reserving 1 1/2 cups of the liquid.

For the vinaigrette, pour the poaching liquid into a bowl. Drizzle in the oil gradually, whisking constantly. Season with salt and pepper.

For the salad, divide the endive evenly among 8 salad plates, fanning out the leaves. Top with equal portions of arugula. Sprinkle with the cheese. Cut the pears lengthwise into halves. Remove the cores with a melon baller. Arrange 2 pear halves over the arugula on each plate. Drizzle with the vinaigrette.

YIELD: 8 SERVINGS

GOURMET MESCLUN WITH RASPBERRY VINAIGRETTE

12 cups mesclun salad mix, or 1 head green leaf lettuce, torn into pieces
1 Granny Smith apple, cut into thin wedges
8 to 10 large strawberries, sliced
8 ounces feta cheese, crumbled
1/2 cup walnuts or pine nuts
Raspberry Vinaigrette (below)

Toss the mesclun, apple, strawberries, feta cheese and walnuts in a large salad bowl. Serve the Raspberry Vinaigrette on the side.

Note: Use your egg slicer to create perfect strawberry slices. This also works well on mushrooms and kiwifruit.

YIELD: 8 SERVINGS

RASPBERRY VINAIGRETTE

1/2 cup raspberry vinegar
4 teaspoons honey
1 tablespoon Dijon mustard
2 garlic cloves, minced
1/2 cup olive oil
1/2 cup vegetable oil
Salt and pepper to taste

Combine the vinegar, honey, Dijon mustard and garlic in a bowl. Whisk in the oils slowly until the vinaigrette is slightly thickened and emulsified. Season with salt and pepper.

YIELD: 1 1/2 CUPS

NEARLY CLASSIC CAESAR SALAD

CAESAR DRESSING
1 (2-ounce) can oil-packed anchovies
2 tablespoons freshly grated Parmesan cheese
1 tablespoon minced garlic
1 tablespoon fresh lemon juice
1 1/2 teaspoons red wine vinegar
1 1/2 teaspoons Worcestershire sauce
1 1/2 teaspoons Dijon mustard
1/2 teaspoon freshly ground pepper
1 cup olive oil
1/2 cup water

SALAD
2 heads romaine, torn into bite-size pieces
1 small head radicchio, thinly sliced
2 tablespoons freshly grated Parmesan cheese
2 cups croutons

For the dressing, combine the anchovies and their oil, cheese and garlic in a food processor or blender and process for 15 seconds. Add the lemon juice, vinegar, Worcestershire sauce, Dijon mustard and pepper and process for 15 seconds. Scrape down the side of the container. Process for 5 seconds. Add the olive oil and water in a slow, steady stream, processing constantly; set aside.

For the salad, combine the lettuce and radicchio in a large bowl. Add 1 cup of the dressing and toss well to coat all the leaves. Divide the salad among 6 plates. Sprinkle evenly with the cheese and croutons.

NOTE: May prepare the dressing up to 2 weeks ahead. Store in the refrigerator.

YIELD: 6 SERVINGS

GREEK SALAD

5 tomatoes, peeled, quartered
2 medium green bell peppers, sliced
2 cucumbers, peeled, sliced
1 cup crumbled feta cheese
4 green onions with tops, chopped
16 to 18 pitted black olives
1 tablespoon minced garlic
3 tablespoons olive oil
3 tablespoons wine vinegar
Salt and freshly ground pepper to taste
Oregano to taste

Toss the tomatoes, bell peppers, cucumbers, cheese, green onions, olives and garlic in a bowl. Drizzle the olive oil and vinegar over the vegetables. Season with salt and pepper. Toss to combine. Sprinkle with oregano.

YIELD: 6 SERVINGS

ASIAN SLAW

2 (3-ounce) packages beef-flavor ramen noodles
1 pound coleslaw mix (chopped or shredded)
1 cup sliced almonds, toasted
1 cup sunflower seeds
1 bunch green onions, chopped
3/4 cup vegetable oil
1/2 cup sugar
1/3 cup white vinegar

Remove the flavor packets from the noodles; set aside. Crush the noodles and place in the bottom of a large bowl. Top with the coleslaw mix, almonds, sunflower seeds and green onions. Whisk the contents of the flavor packets, oil, sugar and vinegar in a bowl. Pour over the layered slaw. Chill, covered, for 24 hours. Toss before serving.

YIELD: 8 TO 10 SERVINGS

HEARTS OF PALM SALAD

DRESSING
1/3 cup extra-virgin olive oil
2 to 3 tablespoons red wine vinegar
3/4 teaspoon salt
1/4 teaspoon salad herbs

SALAD
1 garlic clove, halved
1 (14-ounce) can hearts of palm, drained, chilled
12 cups mixed salad greens
2 cups cherry tomatoes, halved
3 tablespoons freshly grated Parmesan cheese
Freshly ground pepper to taste

For the dressing, combine the olive oil, vinegar, salt and salad herbs in a bowl; set aside.

For the salad, rub the inside of a wooden salad bowl with the garlic pieces; discard the garlic. Slice the hearts of palm into 1-inch pieces. Toss the hearts of palm, salad greens and tomatoes in the salad bowl. Sprinkle with the cheese. Pour the dressing over the salad and toss again. Grind the pepper over the top.

YIELD: 8 SERVINGS

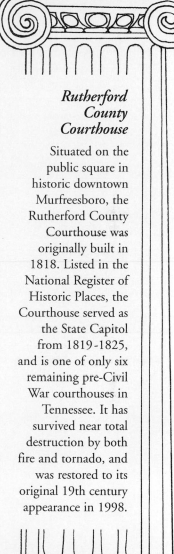

Rutherford County Courthouse

Situated on the public square in historic downtown Murfreesboro, the Rutherford County Courthouse was originally built in 1818. Listed in the National Register of Historic Places, the Courthouse served as the State Capitol from 1819-1825, and is one of only six remaining pre-Civil War courthouses in Tennessee. It has survived near total destruction by both fire and tornado, and was restored to its original 19th century appearance in 1998.

CRUNCHY ROMAINE SALAD

1 head romaine or green leaf lettuce
1 bunch broccoli, stems removed
1 bunch green onions, chopped
1 (11-ounce) can mandarin oranges, drained
6 tablespoons unsalted butter
2 (3-ounce) packages ramen noodles, flavor packets discarded
1 cup chopped walnuts
1 cup vegetable oil
1 cup sugar
1/2 cup red wine vinegar
3 teaspoons soy sauce
Pepper to taste

Tear the romaine into bite-size pieces; place in a large salad bowl. Cut the broccoli florets into small pieces and add to the bowl. Fold in the green onions and mandarin oranges.

Heat the butter in a small skillet over medium heat. Break apart the ramen noodles. Sauté the walnuts and noodles in the butter until golden brown. Stir into the lettuce mixture.

Combine the oil, sugar, vinegar, soy sauce and pepper in a jar with a tight-fitting lid. Shake vigorously to mix well. Chill until serving time. Pour over the salad immediately before serving, tossing to coat well.

YIELD: 8 SERVINGS

BROCCOLI SALAD

The dressing goes a long way! If you double the recipe, there is no need to double the dressing. This salad may be made the night before.

3 stalks broccoli
4 ribs celery, chopped
2/3 cup raisins
10 slices bacon, crisp-cooked, crumbled
1/2 cup chopped red onion
3 tablespoons sunflower seeds
1 cup mayonnaise
1/2 cup sugar
3 tablespoons vinegar

Remove the broccoli florets. Peel and thinly slice the broccoli stems. Combine the broccoli florets and stems, celery, raisins, bacon, onion and sunflower seeds in a bowl. Combine the mayonnaise, sugar and vinegar in a small bowl. Add to the broccoli mixture and toss to combine.

YIELD: 10 TO 12 SERVINGS

Children's Advocacy Center

Through donations of time and funding, the JLM assists with the day-to-day operation of the Children's Advocacy Center. The CAC is a nonprofit agency that provides a child-friendly environment where victims of alleged abuse can be interviewed and counseled by caring, well-trained professionals. The JLM's involvement in the Center began during President Claudia Hunter's term and continued during Lucinda Lea's tenure, becoming a vital community resource for Rutherford County's children.

FRENCH POTATO SALAD

3 pounds small red and white potatoes
2 teaspoons salt
1/4 cup dry white wine or chicken broth
1/4 cup white wine vinegar or cider vinegar
1 tablespoon Dijon mustard
3/4 teaspoon freshly ground pepper
1/3 cup olive oil
4 scallions, chopped
1/4 cup flat-leaf parsley leaves
3 tablespoons chopped fresh basil

Combine the potatoes and 1 teaspoon of the salt in a large saucepan. Add enough water to cover the potatoes. Bring to a boil. Reduce the heat to low. Simmer, covered, for 15 minutes or until tender; drain. Let the potatoes stand until they are cool enough to handle but still warm. Cut the potatoes into halves (or quarters if they are large). Combine the warm potatoes and wine in a bowl, tossing gently until coated. Let stand until completely cool and the wine is absorbed, stirring gently a few times; set aside.

Whisk the vinegar, Dijon mustard, pepper and remaining 1 teaspoon salt in a small bowl until smooth. Whisk in the olive oil gradually until blended. Add to the potatoes. Toss gently to coat. Let stand for 2 hours or until the dressing is absorbed, stirring a few times. (May be prepared up to 1 day ahead at this point. Store, covered, in the refrigerator. Bring to room temperature before serving.)

Stir in the scallions, parsley and basil up to 1 hour before serving. Spoon into a serving bowl.

YIELD: 12 SERVINGS

CASHEW CHICKEN SALAD

4 cups cubed cooked chicken
1 cup chopped celery
$1/2$ cup chopped green bell pepper
1 (4-ounce) jar diced pimentos, drained
$1/2$ cup mayonnaise
$1/3$ cup heavy cream
$1/4$ cup sour cream
3 tablespoons thinly sliced green onions
2 tablespoons minced fresh parsley
1 garlic clove, minced
$1^1/2$ teaspoons lemon juice
$1^1/2$ teaspoons tarragon vinegar or cider vinegar
$1/2$ teaspoon salt
$1/8$ teaspoon black pepper
$3/4$ cup salted cashews
Leaf lettuce and additional cashews (optional)

Combine the chicken, celery, bell pepper and pimentos in a large bowl and mix well; set aside.

Combine the mayonnaise, heavy cream, sour cream, green onions, parsley, garlic, lemon juice, vinegar, salt and pepper in a blender and process until well blended. Pour over the chicken mixture and toss to coat. Chill, covered, until ready to serve.

Fold in $3/4$ cup cashews just before serving. Serve in a lettuce-lined bowl garnished with additional cashews.

YIELD: 6 SERVINGS

BREAKFAST NOOK NIBBLES

brunch and breads

As the party begins, guests tend to gather
in the kitchen. Middle Tennessee
homeowners know the importance of this
room and decorate it for what it is—
the most popular room in the house.
Our guests gather around the island where
they smell the coffee brewing and hear
the bacon sizzling—wonderful accompaniments
to the delicious tastes to come.

FRESH VEGETABLE FRITTATA

Sausage makes a great addition to this recipe. Just cook the sausage, drain, and add as a layer.

1 large red bell pepper, chopped
1 cup sliced fresh mushrooms
1^1/2 cups shredded Swiss cheese
4 ounces fresh asparagus, cut into 1-inch pieces
7 eggs, lightly beaten
^{1}/2 cup mayonnaise
2 tablespoons chopped fresh basil
^{1}/2 teaspoon salt

Layer the bell pepper, mushrooms and ^{3}/4 cup of the cheese in a greased 9-inch deep-dish pie plate. Top with the asparagus and remaining ^{3}/4 cup cheese. Combine the eggs, mayonnaise, basil and salt in a bowl and mix well. Pour evenly over the layered ingredients.

Bake at 375 degrees for 35 minutes or until a knife inserted in the center comes out clean. Let stand for 5 minutes. Serve hot or at room temperature.

YIELD: 8 SERVINGS

TOMATO TART

1 unbaked (9-inch) deep-dish pie shell
3 medium tomatoes, thickly sliced
1/2 cup chopped green onions
1/2 teaspoon salt
1/2 teaspoon chopped fresh basil
1/4 teaspoon pepper
2 cups shredded sharp Cheddar cheese
1/2 cup mayonnaise

Bake the pie shell at 425 degrees for 5 minutes. Remove from the oven. Prick with a fork in several places. Reduce the oven temperature to 400 degrees.

Arrange the tomatoes in the pie shell. Combine the green onions, salt, basil and pepper in a bowl. Sprinkle over the tomatoes. Combine the cheese and mayonnaise in a bowl. Spread over the top.

Bake at 400 degrees for 35 minutes. Cool completely before cutting.

NOTE: If the tomatoes are very juicy, drain the slices on paper towels before placing them in the pie shell.

YIELD: 6 TO 8 SERVINGS

SAUSAGE STRATA

2 pounds bulk pork sausage
2 tablespoons prepared yellow mustard
4 cups milk
5 eggs
1 tablespoon Worcestershire sauce
12 slices bread, crusts removed
Nutmeg to taste
2 cups shredded Cheddar cheese

Brown the sausage in a skillet, stirring until crumbly; drain. Stir in the prepared yellow mustard; set aside. Combine the milk, eggs and Worcestershire sauce in a bowl; set aside.

Arrange the bread slices over the bottom of a greased 3-quart shallow baking dish. Sprinkle with nutmeg. Layer the sausage mixture and cheese $1/2$ at a time over the bread. Pour the milk mixture evenly over the top. Place the baking dish on a baking sheet.

Bake at 350 degrees for 45 minutes or until a knife inserted into the center comes out clean. Let stand for a few minutes before serving.

YIELD: 6 SERVINGS

Camp Forget Me Not

Each summer, JLM volunteers work to support trained staff members of the local hospice as they gather children together who have recently lost a loved one. The volunteers help to foster a caring and loving atmosphere by helping children K-6th grade enjoy a fun weekend camp that will advance the healing process of each child.

SCRAMBLED EGGS WITH SMOKED SALMON AND DILL

8 eggs
4 ounces cream cheese, cut into cubes
4 ounces smoked salmon, cut into thin strips
1 tablespoon chopped fresh dillweed
1/2 teaspoon salt
1/4 teaspoon freshly ground pepper
1 tablespoon unsalted butter

Beat the eggs in a large bowl until fluffy. Add the cream cheese, smoked salmon, dillweed, salt and pepper. Whisk to mix well. Melt the butter in a skillet over medium heat. Pour in the egg mixture. Cook for about 8 minutes or until the eggs achieve desired degree of doneness, stirring constantly to prevent the eggs from sticking. Serve immediately with toast.

YIELD: 6 SERVINGS

MAPLE MUSTARD-GLAZED CANADIAN BACON

1 1/2 tablespoons Dijon mustard
2 teaspoons pure maple syrup
Cayenne pepper to taste
12 ounces thinly sliced Canadian bacon (about 18 slices)

Combine the Dijon mustard, maple syrup and cayenne pepper in a small bowl and mix well. Arrange the Canadian bacon in a single layer on the rack of a broiler pan or in a 10×15-inch baking pan. Brush 1 side of each bacon slice generously with the mustard mixture.

Broil about 4 inches from the heat source for 3 minutes. Turn the bacon over. Broil for 3 to 4 minutes or just until lightly browned around the edges.

YIELD: 6 SERVINGS

CHEDDAR GRITS SOUFFLÉ

1 cup quick-cooking grits
3 cups water
1/4 teaspoon salt
3 cups shredded sharp Cheddar cheese
1/2 cup (1 stick) butter, softened
4 eggs, lightly beaten
1 cup milk
Garlic powder to taste (optional)

Cook the grits with the water and salt according to the package directions. Stir in the cheese, butter, eggs, milk and garlic powder; mix well. Pour into a lightly greased 7×11-inch baking dish. Bake at 350 degrees for 45 minutes or until a knife inserted near the center comes out clean.

YIELD: 8 TO 10 SERVINGS

GORGONZOLA GRITS

2 (14-ounce) cans fat-free chicken broth
3/4 cup quick-cooking grits
4 ounces crumbled Gorgonzola cheese
1/3 cup fat-free sour cream
1/4 teaspoon nutmeg
1/4 teaspoon freshly ground pepper
1/4 teaspoon garlic powder (optional)

Bring the broth to a boil in a medium saucepan. Add the grits gradually, stirring constantly. Reduce the heat to low. Simmer, covered, for 5 minutes or until thick, stirring occasionally. Remove from the heat. Stir in the cheese, sour cream, nutmeg, pepper and garlic powder. Serve immediately.

YIELD: 8 SERVINGS

HOT CURRIED FRUIT SALAD

1 (29-ounce) can pear halves
1 (29-ounce) can peach halves
1 (20-ounce) can pineapple chunks
1 (17-ounce) can apricots
1 (17-ounce) can Royal Anne light sweet cherries
1 (11-ounce) can mandarin oranges
$1/2$ cup golden raisins, soaked in hot water to soften
$3/4$ cup sugar
3 tablespoons butter
3 tablespoons flour
$1/4$ teaspoon salt
$1/2$ to 1 teaspoon curry powder
$1/2$ cup white wine

Drain all the fruit, reserving the juice. Combine the pears, peaches, pineapple, apricots, cherries, oranges and raisins in a large bowl and mix well. Combine $3/4$ cup reserved fruit juice, sugar, butter, flour and salt in a saucepan. Cook until thickened and almost boiling, stirring constantly. Fold the sauce into the fruit mixture. Stir in the curry powder and wine. Let stand for 3 hours.

Pour into a greased baking dish. Bake at 350 degrees for 30 minutes or until bubbly. Serve warm.

YIELD: 8 TO 10 SERVINGS

MIXED FRUIT GRANOLA

Serve with vanilla yogurt for a creamy, healthy treat.

6 cups rolled oats
^{1}/$_2$ cup wheat germ
^{1}/$_2$ cup sunflower seeds
^{1}/$_2$ cup pecans, chopped
^{1}/$_4$ cup sesame seeds
^{1}/$_2$ cup honey
2 tablespoons vegetable oil
1^1/$_2$ teaspoons cinnamon
1^1/$_2$ teaspoons vanilla extract
1^1/$_2$ cups mixed dried fruit, chopped

Combine the oats, wheat germ, sunflower seeds, pecans, sesame seeds, honey, oil, cinnamon and vanilla in a bowl. Spread onto 2 baking sheets coated with nonstick cooking spray.

Bake at 350 degrees for 25 to 30 minutes, stirring 3 times during baking. Cool completely. Stir in the dried fruit. Store in an airtight container in the refrigerator.

YIELD: ABOUT 8^1/$_2$ CUPS

CHAMPAGNE POACHED PEARS

8 Bosc or Bartlett pears
1 (750-milliliter) bottle Champagne
2 quarts orange juice
1 cinnamon stick
5 whole cloves

Peel and core the pears, leaving the stems intact. Cut a thin slice from the bottom of each pear, forming a flat base. Place the pears upright in a Dutch oven. Pour the Champagne and orange juice over the pears. Add the cinnamon stick and cloves to the pot.

Bring to a boil. Reduce the heat to low. Simmer for 15 minutes or until the pears are tender. Remove the pears from the cooking liquid and serve warm. Garnish with strips of orange and lemon zest.

YIELD: 8 SERVINGS

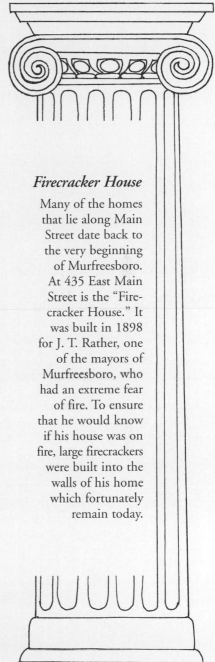

Firecracker House

Many of the homes that lie along Main Street date back to the very beginning of Murfreesboro. At 435 East Main Street is the "Firecracker House." It was built in 1898 for J. T. Rather, one of the mayors of Murfreesboro, who had an extreme fear of fire. To ensure that he would know if his house was on fire, large firecrackers were built into the walls of his home which fortunately remain today.

SIX-GRAIN PECAN PANCAKES WITH APPLE CIDER SYRUP

SYRUP

3 cups apple cider
2 whole allspice
2 whole cloves
1 cinnamon stick
3/4 cup light corn syrup
1/4 cup packed light brown sugar
1/8 teaspoon salt
1/4 cup (1/2 stick) unsalted butter

PANCAKES

1/2 cup each cornmeal, rolled oats,
    whole wheat flour, rye flour, wheat
    bran and flax seeds
1 tablespoon baking powder
1 1/2 teaspoons baking soda
3/4 teaspoon salt
3 cups buttermilk
3 eggs
3/4 cup honey
1/2 cup (1 stick) unsalted butter,
    melted, cooled
1 cup pecan pieces, toasted

For the syrup, combine the cider, allspice, cloves and cinnamon stick in a small nonreactive saucepan. Bring to a boil over medium heat. Reduce the heat to low. Simmer for 20 minutes or until the cider reduces to 1 cup. Stir in the corn syrup, brown sugar and salt. Return to a simmer. Whisk in the butter until it melts. Strain the syrup to remove the spices. Keep warm or chill, covered, for up to 2 weeks.

For the pancakes, combine the cornmeal, oats, whole wheat flour, rye flour, wheat bran, flax seeds, baking powder, baking soda and salt in a large bowl and mix well. Whisk the buttermilk, eggs, honey and butter in a bowl. Add to the flour mixture and mix just until combined. (Do not overmix or the pancakes will be tough. A few lumps are fine.) Stir in the pecans gently.

For each pancake, pour a scant 1/2 cup batter onto a hot griddle over medium-high heat. Cook for 2 to 3 minutes or until bubbles appear on the surface and the underside is browned. Turn the pancake. Cook until browned. Serve with the cider syrup.

NOTE: May also serve the pancakes with warm applesauce.

YIELD: 4 TO 6 SERVINGS

PERFECT PANCAKES

1 cup flour
2 teaspoons sugar
1/2 teaspoon salt
1/2 teaspoon baking powder
1/4 teaspoon baking soda
3/4 cup buttermilk
1/4 cup (or more) milk
1 egg
2 tablespoons butter, melted

Combine the flour, sugar, salt, baking powder and baking soda in a bowl. Combine the buttermilk, milk, egg and butter in a separate bowl. Add to the flour mixture and mix just until combined. (Do not overmix.) Stir in an additional 1 to 2 tablespoons milk if the batter is too thick.

For each pancake, pour a scant 1/4 cup batter onto a hot, lightly greased griddle. Cook until bubbles appear on the surface and the underside is browned. Turn the pancake. Cook until browned.

YIELD: 8 TO 10 PANCAKES

BREAKFAST BUTTERS

A simple addition to a softened stick of butter can make the ordinary extraordinary. For a flavorful change, try adding one of these ingredients to a softened stick of butter. Mix well in a small bowl and enjoy.

3/4 cup pure maple syrup
1 tablespoon brown sugar and 1 teaspoon cinnamon
1/2 teaspoon orange zest
1/2 teaspoon lemon zest
1/3 cup finely chopped toasted pecans and 2 tablespoons honey

To create perfect butter balls, use a small melon baller that has been dipped in very hot water. Drop the balls into iced water until ready to serve.

BLUEBERRY AND POPPY SEED BRUNCH CAKE

CAKE
2/3 cup sugar
1/2 cup (1 stick) butter, softened
2 teaspoons grated lemon zest
1 egg
1 1/2 cups flour
2 tablespoons poppy seeds
1/2 teaspoon baking soda
1/4 teaspoon salt
1/2 cup sour cream

FILLING
2 cups fresh blueberries, or frozen
    blueberries, thawed and drained on
    paper towels
1/3 cup sugar
2 teaspoons flour
1/4 teaspoon nutmeg

GLAZE
1/3 cup confectioners' sugar
1 to 2 teaspoons milk

For the cake, beat the sugar and butter in a large mixing bowl until light and fluffy. Add the lemon zest and egg. Beat at medium speed for 2 minutes. Combine the flour, poppy seeds, baking soda and salt in a bowl. Add to the butter mixture alternately with the sour cream, mixing well after each addition. Spread the batter over the bottom and 1 inch up the side of a greased and floured 9- or 10-inch springform pan, making sure the batter on the side is 1/4 inch thick; set aside.

For the filling, combine the blueberries, sugar, flour and nutmeg in a medium bowl. Spoon over the batter. Bake at 350 degrees for 45 to 55 minutes or until the cake is lightly browned. Cool on a wire rack. Remove the side of the pan.

For the glaze, combine the confectioners' sugar and enough of the milk in a small bowl until smooth and a drizzling consistency. Drizzle over the warm cake.

YIELD: 8 SERVINGS

CRANBERRY CREAM CHEESE RING

You may use cranberries in this recipe during the holiday season and raisins the rest of the year.

> *1 cup dried cranberries*
> *2 dozen frozen dinner rolls, thawed but cold*
> *¹/4 cup (¹/2 stick) butter, melted*
> *1 cup sugar*
> *6 ounces cream cheese, softened*
> *3 tablespoons fresh orange juice*
> *1 tablespoon grated orange zest*
> *1 tablespoon grated lemon zest*
> *1 cup confectioners' sugar*
> *5 teaspoons lemon juice*

Press about 1 teaspoon of the cranberries into each thawed roll. Place the rolls in a greased bundt pan.

Combine the butter, ¹/2 cup of the sugar, cream cheese and orange juice in a bowl and blend well. Pour over the rolls. Cover with plastic wrap. Let rise in a warm place until doubled in bulk.

Combine the remaining ¹/2 cup sugar, orange zest, lemon zest and any remaining cranberries in a bowl. Sprinkle over the rolls. Bake at 350 degrees for 25 to 30 minutes or until the rolls in the center are done. Invert onto a serving plate.

Combine the confectioners' sugar and lemon juice in a bowl. Drizzle over the warm rolls.

YIELD: 24 SERVINGS

BANANA BREAD

Warm your bread knife over a burner before you slice hot bread. This will prevent the bread from compressing and tearing.

1/2 cup (1 stick) butter, softened
1 cup sugar
2 eggs
1 teaspoon vanilla extract
1 cup mashed bananas
1/2 cup sour cream
11/2 cups flour
1 teaspoon baking soda
1/2 teaspoon salt

Cream the butter and sugar in a mixing bowl until light and fluffy. Beat in the eggs and vanilla. Add the bananas and sour cream; mix well. Add the flour, baking soda and salt. Beat for 1 minute. Pour into a greased and floured 5×9-inch loaf pan.

Bake at 350 degrees for 1 hour or until the loaf tests done. Remove to a wire rack to cool.

VARIATIONS: This is a great recipe for muffins. Fill greased and floured muffin cups 2/3 full. Bake at 350 degrees for 20 to 22 minutes.

NOTE: May substitute any flavor pie filling for the mashed bananas. Apricot pie filling is especially delicious.

YIELD: 12 SERVINGS

LEMON POPPY SEED SCONES

2 cups flour
2 tablespoons sugar
2 teaspoons baking powder
1/2 teaspoon salt
1/4 teaspoon baking soda
1/3 cup butter, cut into pieces
1/2 cup buttermilk
1 egg, lightly beaten
2 teaspoons grated lemon zest
1 teaspoon poppy seeds
1 cup sifted confectioners' sugar
1 1/2 tablespoons fresh lemon juice

Combine the flour, sugar, baking powder, salt and baking soda in a bowl. Cut in the butter until crumbly. Stir in the buttermilk, egg, lemon zest and poppy seeds until the dry ingredients are moistened.

Knead the dough 5 to 6 times on a lightly floured surface. Divide the dough into halves. Roll or pat each half into a 6-inch circle. Cut each circle into 8 wedges. Place 1 inch apart on a lightly greased baking sheet. Bake at 425 degrees for 12 to 15 minutes or until lightly browned.

Combine the confectioners' sugar and lemon juice in a bowl. Lightly spread over the scones to glaze.

YIELD: 16 SCONES

TENNESSEE SPICE MUFFINS

1 cup (2 sticks) butter or margarine, softened
2 cups sugar
2 eggs
2 cups applesauce (preferably unsweetened)
1 tablespoon cinnamon
2 teaspoons allspice
1 teaspoon ground cloves
4 cups flour
2 teaspoons baking soda
1 teaspoon salt
1 cup nuts, chopped
Confectioners' sugar

Cream the butter and sugar in a mixing bowl until light and fluffy. Add the eggs 1 at a time, mixing well after each addition. Add the applesauce, cinnamon, allspice and cloves; mix well. Sift the flour, baking soda and salt together. Add to the applesauce mixture and beat well. Stir in the nuts. Spoon the batter into lightly greased miniature muffin cups.

Bake at 350 degrees for 8 to 10 minutes or until the muffins test done. Remove to a wire rack to cool. Sprinkle with confectioners' sugar.

NOTE: May refrigerate the batter in an airtight container for up to 2 weeks. Baked muffins freeze well. Reheat before serving.

YIELD: 7 DOZEN MUFFINS

YEAST ROLLS

1/2 cup (1 stick) butter, softened
1/2 cup shortening
1 cup sugar
11/2 teaspoons salt
2 envelopes dry yeast
2 cups warm (105-degree) water
1 tablespoon sugar
6 cups flour
2 eggs, beaten

Microwave the softened butter, shortening, 1 cup sugar and salt in a microwave-safe bowl on High until the butter and shortening melt. Cool; set aside.

Dissolve the yeast in the warm water in a small bowl. Sprinkle 1 tablespoon sugar over the top. Let stand for 5 minutes or until foamy.

Add 1 cup of the flour to the cooled butter mixture; mix well. Stir in the eggs and yeast mixture. Add the remaining 5 cups flour, 1 cup at a time, mixing well after each addition. Cover the bowl with plastic wrap. Chill for 4 to 12 hours. (The dough should double in bulk.) Remove the dough from the refrigerator 3 hours before baking. Shape as desired in the Variations below. Bake at 400 degrees for 12 to 15 minutes or until lightly browned.

NOTE: May chill the dough, covered, for up to 1 week.

YIELD: 3 DOZEN ROLLS

VARIATIONS: **Parker House Rolls:** Roll out 1/2 of the dough at a time to a 1/2-inch thickness on a lightly floured surface. Cut into 3-inch circles. Brush each circle with melted butter. Fold each circle in half so the butter is on the inside. Place in greased 9×13-inch baking pans. Let rise in a warm place for 3 hours or until doubled in bulk. Bake as directed above. **Crescent Rolls:** Roll out 1/3 of the dough at a time into a circle on a lightly floured surface. Cut each circle into 12 wedges. Roll up the wedges from the wide ends. Shape into crescents on a greased baking sheet. Let rise in a warm place for 3 hours or until doubled in bulk. Bake as directed above. **Cloverleaf Rolls:** Shape the dough into 1-inch balls. For each roll, place 3 balls in a greased muffin cup. Let rise in a warm place for 3 hours or until doubled in bulk. Bake as directed above.

SIDEBOARD SELECTIONS

side dishes

Our traditions tell us that there is
no such thing as too much food.
Our stunning sideboard allows a bountiful
array of complements to our
main dish to be admired and enjoyed.

ARTICHOKES AND OLIVES

1/2 cup olive oil
1/2 cup chopped onion
1/2 cup chopped carrots
2 ribs celery, chopped
2 bay leaves
1/4 cup chopped garlic
1/2 teaspoon crushed red pepper
1 cup chicken broth
1/2 cup white wine
1/4 cup lemon juice
2 pounds canned artichoke quarters
Salt and pepper to taste
1/2 cup sun-dried tomatoes, chopped
1/2 cup pitted kalamata olives, chopped
1/4 cup fresh thyme leaves
2 tablespoons chopped fresh parsley
1 tablespoon fresh rosemary leaves, chopped

Heat the olive oil in a heavy pan over medium heat. Add the onion, carrots and celery. Cook until the vegetables are tender. Stir in the bay leaves, garlic and red pepper. Cook for 1 minute. Add the broth, wine and lemon juice. Bring to a boil. Reduce the heat to low. Add the artichokes and season with salt and pepper. Stir in the sun-dried tomatoes and olives. Simmer until the artichokes are tender, stirring occasionally. Remove and discard the bay leaves. Taste and adjust the seasonings. Stir in the thyme, parsley and rosemary. Serve immediately.

YIELD: 8 SERVINGS

ASPARAGUS GOAT CHEESE SOUFFLÉ

2 tablespoons butter
2 tablespoons chopped onion
1 pound fresh asparagus, cut into 1-inch pieces (about 2 cups)
1/2 teaspoon salt
2 tablespoons water
6 eggs
1/3 cup heavy cream
1/2 teaspoon salt
Pepper to taste
2 tablespoons butter
6 ounces goat cheese

Melt 2 tablespoons butter in a saucepan. Add the onion. Sauté until tender and lightly browned. Add the asparagus and 1/2 teaspoon salt. Cook for 1 minute, tossing constantly. Add the water and cover the pan. Steam for 1 to 2 minutes, shaking the pan constantly. Uncover the pan. Cook until the liquid has evaporated. Cool slightly.

Beat the eggs, cream, 1/2 teaspoon salt and pepper in a bowl. Melt 2 tablespoons butter in a 10×10-inch ovenproof baking dish. Pour in the egg mixture. Bake at 425 degrees for 3 minutes or until the egg layer is set. Arrange the asparagus mixture in a single layer over the eggs.

Bake at 425 degrees for 5 minutes. Remove from the oven. Top with the cheese. Bake for 10 minutes or until the eggs are puffed and the cheese is lightly browned.

NOTE: May substitute 1 1/2 cups shredded Muenster cheese for the goat cheese.

YIELD: 4 SERVINGS

ASPARAGUS VINAIGRETTE

1 pound fresh asparagus, trimmed
1/3 cup tarragon vinegar
1 tablespoon lemon juice
2 green onions, chopped
1 garlic clove, pressed
1/2 teaspoon tarragon, crushed
1/2 teaspoon Dijon mustard

Pour enough water in a pan to cover the asparagus. Bring to a boil. Add the asparagus. Cook for 5 minutes; drain. Arrange the asparagus in a shallow dish. Combine the vinegar, lemon juice, green onions, garlic, tarragon and Dijon mustard in a bowl and mix well. Pour over the asparagus. Chill, covered, for 8 hours. Remove the asparagus from the marinade. Serve in bundles tied with strips of lemon zest if desired.

YIELD: 4 SERVINGS

SESAME ROASTED ASPARAGUS

1 pound fresh asparagus, trimmed
2 tablespoons dry sherry
2 tablespoons vegetable oil
1 tablespoon soy sauce
1 tablespoon sesame seeds
1 teaspoon sesame oil
Pinch of hot red pepper flakes

Arrange the asparagus in a single layer in a large baking dish. Whisk the sherry, vegetable oil, soy sauce, sesame seeds, sesame oil and red pepper in a small bowl. Drizzle over the asparagus, rolling the spears to coat them evenly. Roast at 450 degrees for 6 to 8 minutes or until tender. Taste and adjust the seasonings. Serve immediately.

YIELD: 4 SERVINGS

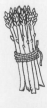

BROCCOLI WITH TANGY SAUCE

1 bunch broccoli, separated into florets
2 tablespoons unsalted butter
2 tablespoons extra-virgin olive oil
1 tablespoon cider vinegar
1 1/2 teaspoons Worcestershire sauce
1 teaspoon Dijon mustard
Salt and pepper to taste

Blanch the broccoli in a pot of rapidly boiling water for 2 to 3 minutes; drain. Rinse under cold water until cooled; drain and set aside.

Combine the butter, olive oil, vinegar, Worcestershire sauce, Dijon mustard, salt and pepper in a saucepan. Heat until the butter melts, stirring occasionally. Pour over the cooked broccoli in a bowl.

YIELD: 4 TO 6 SERVINGS

SAVORY GREEN BEANS

2 pounds fresh green beans, trimmed
1/4 cup (1/2 stick) butter
3 green onions, sliced
2 garlic cloves, minced
1 1/2 teaspoons Creole seasoning
1/2 teaspoon freshly ground pepper
1/2 teaspoon dillweed

Pour water into a Dutch oven to a 1-inch depth. Bring to a boil. Add the green beans. Reduce the heat to low. Simmer, covered, for 10 minutes or until the beans are tender-crisp; drain. Plunge the beans into a bowl of ice water until cooled; drain and set aside.

Melt the butter in the Dutch oven over medium heat. Add the green onions, garlic, Creole seasoning, pepper and dillweed. Cook until the green onions are tender, stirring constantly. Add the beans. Cook until the beans are heated through.

YIELD: 8 SERVINGS

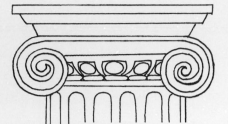

GREEN BEANS WITH CARAMELIZED ONIONS

1 pound fresh green beans, trimmed
2 medium sweet onions, thinly sliced
2 tablespoons butter or margarine
2 tablespoons brown sugar
1 to 2 teaspoons balsamic vinegar (optional)

Cook the beans in a saucepan of boiling water until tender; drain and set aside. Cut the onion slices in half. Cook over medium heat in a nonstick skillet for 8 to 10 minutes. Do not stir. Cook for an additional 5 to 10 minutes or until lightly browned, stirring frequently. Reduce the heat to medium-low. Stir in the butter and brown sugar. Add the green beans. Cook for 5 minutes or until the beans are heated through. Toss with the vinegar.

NOTE: May substitute 1 (28-ounce) can green beans for the fresh beans. Cook until heated through; drain and set aside.

YIELD: 6 TO 8 SERVINGS

Stones River National Battlefield

Although the preserved grounds contain just a token part of the original battlefield, the Stones River battle was one of the fiercest of the Civil War. Union troops made their final stand here, and a total of 81,000 men battled for control of Middle Tennessee. Part of the National Park system, self-guided tours are available which show battlefields, cannons, and ammunition used during the battle.

CIDER BRAISED CABBAGE

Serve this with a rich meat dish. It offers a sharp and tangy contrast!

1 tablespoon olive oil
1/3 cup chopped hickory-smoked bacon
1 small white onion, minced
1 carrot, chopped
1 small head red or green cabbage, halved, cored, thinly sliced
1 cup apple cider
3/4 cup cider vinegar
2 tablespoons sugar
1 bay leaf
5 peppercorns
Salt and freshly ground pepper

Heat the olive oil in a large nonreactive saucepan over medium heat until it ripples. Add the bacon. Cook until browned and crisp. Add the onion and carrot. Cook for 3 to 4 minutes or until tender. Add the cabbage, tossing to coat with the olive oil. Stir in the apple cider, vinegar, sugar, bay leaf and peppercorns. Cook for 2 to 3 minutes or until the cabbage begins to wilt.

Reduce the heat to very low and tightly cover the pan. Braise slowly for 45 to 60 minutes or until the cabbage is very tender. Remove from the heat. Season with salt and ground pepper. Remove and discard the bay leaf. Serve immediately or cool to room temperature and chill, covered, for up to 2 days. Reheat before serving.

YIELD: 6 TO 8 SERVINGS

CARROT SOUFFLÉ

This dish is always a favorite at Thanksgiving and Christmas. It can be served as a dessert or vegetable dish.

> *3 pounds carrots, sliced*
> *1^1/2 cups (3 sticks) butter or margarine*
> *3 cups sugar*
> *6 eggs*
> *^{1}/2 cup flour*
> *1 tablespoon baking powder*
> *^{1}/4 teaspoon cinnamon*
> *Confectioners' sugar*

Cook the carrots in a saucepan of boiling water for 15 minutes or until tender; drain and cool. Combine the carrots, butter, sugar, eggs, flour, baking powder and cinnamon in a food processor and process until smooth, stopping once to scrape down the side of the container. Spoon into 2 lightly greased 1^1/2-quart soufflé or baking dishes. Bake at 350 degrees for 1 hour or until set and lightly browned. Sprinkle with confectioners' sugar. Serve warm.

YIELD: 12 SERVINGS

MOZZARELLA CORN PUDDING

1 (14-ounce) can cream-style corn
1 (14-ounce) can whole kernel corn
1 (8-ounce) package corn muffin mix
1 cup sour cream
$^1/2$ cup (1 stick) butter, melted
2 eggs, lightly beaten
8 ounces shredded mozzarella cheese

Combine the cream-style corn, undrained whole kernel corn, muffin mix, sour cream, butter and eggs in a bowl and mix well. Pour into a 9×13-inch baking dish. Sprinkle the cheese over the top. Bake at 350 degrees for 30 minutes or until the pudding tests done.

YIELD: 6 TO 8 SERVINGS

SOUTHWESTERN SPOON BREAD

1 cup yellow cornmeal
$^1/2$ teaspoon baking soda
1 teaspoon salt
1 (17-ounce) can cream-style corn
$^3/4$ cup milk
$^1/3$ cup vegetable oil
2 eggs, beaten
1 (4-ounce) can chopped mild green chiles
2 cups shredded Monterey Jack cheese

Combine the cornmeal, baking soda and salt in a bowl and mix well. Combine the corn, milk, oil and eggs in a separate bowl. Add to the cornmeal mixture and mix well. Layer the cornmeal batter, chiles and cheese $^1/2$ at a time in a 2-quart round baking dish. Bake at 350 degrees for 45 minutes or until the bread tests done.

YIELD: 4 TO 6 SERVINGS

SAUTÉED GREENS AND GARLIC

3 tablespoons olive oil
6 garlic cloves, minced
Greens (see Note)
Salt and pepper to taste
Lemon juice or balsamic vinegar to taste (optional)

Heat the olive oil in a large nonreactive sauté pan over medium-high heat. Add the garlic and sauté for 1 minute. Add the greens and a few tablespoons water. Season with salt and pepper. Cook, covered, until the greens are tender and wilted, stirring occasionally. (Cooking time varies with the type of greens.) Season with salt, pepper and lemon juice. Serve immediately.

NOTE: Choose one of the greens listed below. Wash greens thoroughly. Remove and discard tough stems before cooking. If the greens will be cooked immediately after washing, do not dry them. The moisture clinging to their leaves helps to cook them. Dry the greens only if they will not be cooked right away.

2 pounds Swiss chard, cut into 2-inch strips
2 pounds broccoli rabe, cut into 2-inch strips
2 pounds bok choy, cut into 2-inch strips
1¹⁄4 pounds spinach
1¹⁄4 pounds kale, cut into 2-inch strips
1¹⁄4 pounds arugula

YIELD: 4 TO 6 SERVINGS

BALSAMIC ROASTED PORTOBELLO MUSHROOMS

These fleshy mushrooms have a great meaty flavor. They're terrific grilled and make a great sandwich!

4 large portobello mushrooms
1/2 cup balsamic vinegar
1/2 cup soy sauce
1/2 cup olive oil
1/2 cup water
1/2 small red onion, minced
2 tablespoons chopped fresh rosemary
1 teaspoon minced garlic
1 teaspoon freshly ground pepper

Remove and discard the mushroom stems. Brush the mushroom caps to remove any dirt. Place the mushroom caps, gill sides up, in a shallow baking dish. Whisk the vinegar, soy sauce, olive oil, water, onion, rosemary, garlic and pepper in a bowl. Pour over the mushrooms, coating them evenly. Chill, covered, for at least 4 hours or up to 2 days.

Roast at 450 degrees for 12 to 15 minutes or until tender and cooked through. Serve immediately.

YIELD: 4 SERVINGS

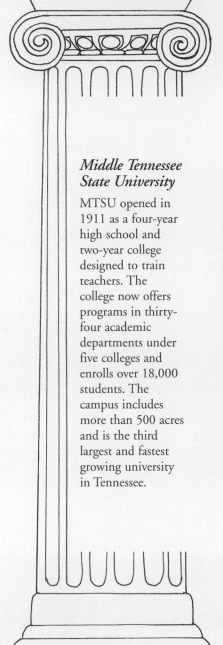

VIDALIA ONION BAKE

4 large Vidalia onions, sliced into rings
1/2 cup (1 stick) unsalted butter, softened
50 butter crackers, crushed
8 ounces shredded Cheddar cheese
Salt to taste
Paprika to taste
1 cup milk
3 eggs, beaten

Middle Tennessee State University

MTSU opened in 1911 as a four-year high school and two-year college designed to train teachers. The college now offers programs in thirty-four academic departments under five colleges and enrolls over 18,000 students. The campus includes more than 500 acres and is the third largest and fastest growing university in Tennessee.

Sauté the onions in 1/4 cup of the butter in a skillet until tender; set aside. Combine the remaining 1/4 cup butter with the cracker crumbs in a bowl. Reserve 1/4 cup of the crumb mixture for the topping. Sprinkle the remaining crumb mixture over the bottom of a greased 9×13-inch baking dish. Top with the onions, cheese, salt and paprika.

Combine the milk and eggs in a bowl and mix well. Pour over the onions and cheese. Top with the reserved crumb mixture. Bake at 350 degrees for 35 to 40 minutes.

NOTE: May substitute any variety of sweet onion for the Vidalia onions.

YIELD: 8 SERVINGS

TWO-POTATO SAUTÉ

2 pounds white-skinned potatoes, peeled, cut into cubes
1¹/2 pounds sweet potatoes, peeled, cut into cubes
7 slices bacon, coarsely chopped
3/4 cup chopped onion
1/2 cup coarsely chopped red bell pepper
1/4 cup heavy cream
Salt and pepper to taste
3 tablespoons chopped flat-leaf parsley

Bring a large pot of salted water to a boil. Add the white potatoes. Cook, partially covered, for 10 minutes or until almost tender. Remove to a large bowl with a slotted spoon; set aside.

Return the water in the pot to a boil. Add the sweet potatoes. Cook until tender; drain. Add to the bowl of white potatoes; set aside.

Cook the bacon in a skillet for 10 minutes or until crisp. Remove to paper towels with a slotted spoon. Pour off all but 1/4 cup of the drippings. Add the onion and bell pepper to the drippings in the pan. Cook for 15 minutes or until tender. Stir in the potatoes and bacon. Cook for 10 minutes. Add the cream. Cook, uncovered, until heated through and the potatoes are coated with sauce. Season with salt and pepper. Sprinkle with the parsley.

YIELD: 8 SERVINGS

GARLIC MASHED POTATOES

2 garlic bulbs
2 tablespoons olive oil
$^1/_4$ cup white vermouth or dry white wine
$^1/_4$ cup low-sodium chicken broth
$3^1/_2$ pounds Yukon gold potatoes, cut into 2-inch pieces
1 cup half-and-half
6 tablespoons butter, softened
Salt and pepper to taste

Peel the loose skin off the garlic bulbs, leaving the cloves attached. Cut $^1/_4$ inch off the top of each bulb. Place the garlic bulbs in a baking dish. Drizzle with the olive oil. Bring the vermouth and broth to a boil in a saucepan. Pour over the garlic. Bake, covered, at 375 degrees for 45 minutes or until tender. Cool slightly. Squeeze the garlic from its peels into a small bowl. Mash with a fork; set aside.

Place the potatoes in a large pot of water. Bring to a boil. Reduce the heat to low. Simmer, partially covered, for 20 minutes or until tender; drain. Return the potatoes to the pot. Heat the half-and-half in a small saucepan until hot. Mash the potatoes. Add the half-and-half and mix well. Stir in the garlic and butter. Season with salt and pepper.

NOTE: Try adding $^1/_8$ teaspoon vinegar to the water when boiling potatoes or rice. The vinegar keeps the starches white and prevents them from getting sticky.

YIELD: 10 SERVINGS

PARMESAN POTATOES

2 pounds new potatoes, cut into quarters or 1^1/2-inch cubes
2 garlic cloves, minced
2 tablespoons butter
1 cup cream
1 cup shredded Parmesan cheese
Salt and white pepper to taste

Place the potatoes and a small amount of water in a microwave-safe bowl. Microwave, covered, for 25 minutes or until fork-tender, stirring twice.

Heat the garlic in the butter in a large skillet until slightly cooked. Stir in the cream gradually. Cook until the sauce begins to thicken. Stir in ^{3}/4 cup of the cheese and the potatoes. Cook until heated through. Season with salt and pepper. Remove the potatoes to a serving bowl. Top with the remaining ^{1}/4 cup cheese. Sprinkle with chopped fresh parsley if desired.

YIELD: 6 TO 8 SERVINGS

ROASTED RED PEPPER POTATO CAKES

1 pound red-skinned potatoes
Pinch of salt
2 tablespoons olive oil
1 cup minced yellow onion
1 tablespoon chopped fresh thyme
1 teaspoon minced garlic
2 red bell peppers, roasted, peeled, chopped
3/4 cup freshly grated Parmesan cheese
1 egg yolk, beaten
Freshly ground pepper to taste
Flour for dusting
1/4 cup olive oil

Combine the potatoes and salt in a saucepan and add enough water to cover the potatoes by 2 inches. Bring to a boil over high heat. Reduce the heat to low. Simmer for 20 minutes or until the potatoes are easily pierced with a fork; drain well. Return the potatoes to the pan over low heat. Toss for 1 minute to evaporate any excess moisture; keep warm.

Heat 2 tablespoons olive oil in a sauté pan over medium-high heat. Add the onion. Cook for 5 minutes or until tender. Add the thyme and garlic. Cook for 2 minutes; set aside.

Mash the potatoes with a sturdy whisk or potato masher. Add the onion mixture, bell peppers, cheese, egg yolk and pepper and mix well with a spoon. Shape into four 5-inch cakes. (May prepare the cakes up to 2 days in advance at this point. Chill, covered, until ready to use.)

Dust both sides of each potato cake lightly with flour. Heat 1/4 cup olive oil in a large sauté pan over medium heat until it ripples. Add the potato cakes carefully. Cook 4 minutes on each side or until lightly browned. Serve hot.

YIELD: 4 SERVINGS

CANDIED SWEET POTATOES

6 medium sweet potatoes (about 4¹/2 pounds)
¹/2 cup plus 2 tablespoons sugar
¹/3 cup packed brown sugar
2 tablespoons flour
1 teaspoon cinnamon
¹/4 teaspoon nutmeg
¹/4 teaspoon allspice
³/4 cup pineapple juice
¹/3 cup light corn syrup
¹/4 cup (¹/2 stick) margarine
2 tablespoons orange juice
¹/2 cup chopped pecans

Cook the sweet potatoes in boiling water in a saucepan for 20 to 25 minutes or until fork-tender; cool. Peel the potatoes and cut lengthwise into ¹/4-inch slices; set aside.

Combine the sugar, brown sugar, flour, cinnamon, nutmeg and allspice in a saucepan. Stir in the pineapple juice, corn syrup, margarine and orange juice. Cook over medium heat for 10 minutes, stirring occasionally.

Layer the potatoes and sugar mixture ¹/2 at a time in a lightly greased 9×13-inch baking dish. Sprinkle with the pecans. Bake at 350 degrees for 30 minutes.

NOTE: Storing potatoes with an apple in the same bag will keep the potatoes from sprouting.

YIELD: 6 SERVINGS

GRILLED VEGETABLES

You can play with the veggies in this recipe and use the ones you like. You can also use different herbs and vinegars.

1 cup vegetable stock or broth
1/4 cup balsamic vinegar
1 tablespoon Dijon mustard
2 teaspoons extra-virgin olive oil
1 teaspoon thyme
Pinch of freshly ground pepper
Zucchini, cut diagonally into 1/4-inch slices
Bell peppers, quartered, seeded
1 small red onion, thickly sliced
1 head endive, quartered
1 small head radicchio, quartered

Combine the stock, vinegar, Dijon mustard, olive oil, thyme and pepper in a large bowl and mix well. Add the zucchini, bell peppers, onion, endive and radicchio. Toss to coat the vegetables with the marinade. Marinate, covered, for about 3 hours.

Grill the vegetables for 1 to 2 minutes per side. Do not allow them to turn black.

YIELD: 4 TO 6 SERVINGS

NUTTED RICE

2 (6-ounce) packages long grain and wild rice mix
Chicken stock
1 cup pecan halves, coarsely chopped
1 cup golden raisins
1/3 cup fresh orange juice
1/4 cup chopped fresh mint
1/4 cup olive oil
4 scallions, thinly sliced
1 1/2 teaspoons salt
Grated zest of 1 large orange
Freshly ground pepper to taste

Prepare the rice according to the package directions substituting chicken stock for the water. Do not overcook the rice.

Remove the rice to a bowl. Add the pecans, raisins, orange juice, mint, olive oil, scallions, salt, orange zest and pepper and toss gently. Taste and adjust the seasonings. Chill, covered, for 2 hours. Serve at room temperature.

YIELD: 8 SERVINGS

ASIAN RICE PILAF

1 (4-ounce) package wild rice
1 onion, chopped
1 cup chopped green bell pepper
2 (4-ounce) cans sliced mushrooms, drained
1/2 cup chopped pimentos
1/2 cup (1 stick) butter
1 (8-ounce) can water chestnuts, drained

Prepare the wild rice according to the package directions; set aside.

Sauté the onion, bell pepper, mushrooms and pimentos in the butter in a skillet. Stir the vegetable mixture and water chestnuts into the cooked rice.

YIELD: 6 SERVINGS

SPINACH RICE WITH PINE NUTS

1 (10-ounce) package frozen chopped spinach, thawed
1/2 cup chopped green onions
1/2 cup (1 stick) butter
4 cups chicken broth
2 cups rice
Salt to taste
1/3 cup grated Parmesan cheese
1/4 cup toasted pine nuts
1/4 cup minced fresh parsley

Sauté the spinach and green onions in the butter in a 3- to 4-quart saucepan for 5 minutes. Stir in the broth, rice and salt. Bring to a boil. Reduce the heat to low. Simmer, tightly covered, for 15 minutes. Remove from the heat. Stir in the cheese, pine nuts and parsley. Fluff and serve.

YIELD: 6 TO 8 SERVINGS

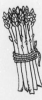

RICE WITH ROASTED POBLANOS AND SPINACH

3 medium poblano chiles
2 cups chicken broth
3/4 teaspoon salt (see Note)
2 tablespoons olive oil
1 1/2 cups rice
1 small onion, chopped
2 garlic cloves, minced
3 cups loosely packed sliced spinach leaves

Roast the chiles directly over a gas flame or broil on a baking sheet in the oven until the skins are blistered and blackened, turning frequently. Place the chiles in a bowl and cover with plastic wrap. Let stand for 5 minutes or until they are cool enough to handle. Remove and discard the skins, stems and seeds. Chop the roasted chiles into 1/4-inch pieces; set aside.

Heat the broth in a small saucepan until steaming. Stir in the salt. Cover and keep warm.

Heat the olive oil in a medium saucepan over medium heat. Add the rice and onion. Cook for 4 to 5 minutes or until the rice turns opaque. Add the garlic. Cook for a few seconds, stirring constantly. Add the warm broth and roasted chiles and stir well, scraping down any rice grains clinging to the side of the pan. Cook, covered, for 15 minutes. Remove from the heat. Distribute the spinach over the rice. Cover and let stand for 5 minutes.

NOTE: If using unsalted chicken broth, increase the salt to 1 1/2 teaspoons.

YIELD: 6 TO 8 SERVINGS

BROCCOLI RISOTTO

1 bunch broccoli
6 cups water
2 tablespoons olive oil
1 cup minced white onion
2 cups arborio rice
1 cup dry white wine
1 teaspoon salt
1/2 teaspoon freshly ground pepper
1 (5-ounce) package boursin cheese with garlic and herbs
1/2 cup freshly grated Parmesan cheese

Cut the broccoli stems and florets into 2-inch pieces. Bring the water to a boil in a saucepan. Add the broccoli. Cook for 3 to 5 minutes or until tender. Remove the broccoli from the pan with a slotted spoon to a bowl of ice water. Let stand until cool; drain. Reserve the cooking liquid. Chop the broccoli finely; set aside.

Heat the olive oil in a nonreactive saucepan over medium heat until it ripples. Add the onion. Cook for 5 minutes or until tender. Add the rice and toss to coat with the oil. Cook for 1 to 2 minutes or until the rice has a nutty aroma, stirring constantly. Add the wine and stir until it is completely absorbed. Add enough of the reserved broccoli cooking liquid to just cover the rice. Bring to a gentle simmer, stirring constantly. Continue adding the liquid a ladleful at a time, stirring after each addition, until the liquid is completely absorbed. (You will not use all of the liquid.) After 20 minutes, the rice should be tender but firm in the center. Stir in the broccoli, salt and pepper. Cook for 3 to 5 minutes, stirring constantly. (Add more liquid if the rice isn't completely cooked or becomes sticky.)

Stir in the boursin and Parmesan cheeses just before serving. The risotto should be creamy but not runny. Taste and adjust the seasonings. Serve immediately.

YIELD: 6 TO 8 SERVINGS

WILD MUSHROOM RISOTTO

4 ounces wild mushrooms, sliced (such as shiitake, portobello, cremini)
4 ounces white button mushrooms, sliced
5 tablespoons unsalted butter
Salt and pepper to taste
1 tablespoon vegetable oil
$1/3$ cup minced onion
$1^1/2$ cups arborio rice
$1/2$ cup white wine
5 cups chicken or beef broth
$1/4$ cup mascarpone cheese
$1/4$ cup grated Parmesan cheese
1 tablespoon chopped fresh parsley

Sauté the mushrooms in 3 tablespoons of the butter in a skillet over medium heat until tender. Season with salt and pepper; set aside.

Heat the oil and the remaining 2 tablespoons butter in a large pot until the butter melts. Add the onion. Sauté until tender. Add the rice and stir to coat with the butter and oil. Cook for 1 minute, stirring constantly. Add the wine and 1 cup of the broth. Simmer until the liquid is almost completely absorbed. Continue adding the broth a ladleful at a time, stirring after each addition, until the broth is completely absorbed. (Stir frequently to prevent the rice from sticking to the bottom of the pot.) When the rice is tender and creamy, add the mascarpone cheese, Parmesan cheese and parsley. Serve immediately.

NOTE: To prevent mushrooms from drying out, store them in a brown paper bag in the refrigerator.

YIELD: 6 SERVINGS

CREAMY MACARONI AND CHEESE

1/3 cup butter
1/3 cup flour
2 2/3 cups milk
1 cup (4 ounces) shredded fontina or Swiss cheese
3/4 cup grated Parmesan cheese
3/4 cup shredded extra-sharp Cheddar cheese
5 ounces Velveeta cheese, cubed
12 ounces elbow macaroni, cooked drained
1/4 teaspoon salt
1/4 teaspoon pepper
1/3 cup crushed melba toasts
1 tablespoon butter, melted

Heat 1/3 cup butter in a skillet over medium heat until melted. Stir in the flour until bubbly. Add the milk, whisking constantly. Cook for 8 minutes or until thickened, stirring constantly. Add all the cheeses. Cook for 3 minutes longer or until the cheeses have melted, stirring frequently. Remove from the heat. Stir in the macaroni, salt and pepper. Spoon into a 2-quart baking dish coated with nonstick cooking spray.

Combine the melba toasts and 1 tablespoon butter in a bowl and mix well. Sprinkle over the macaroni mixture. Bake at 375 degrees for 30 minutes or until bubbly.

YIELD: 12 SERVINGS

BAKED FONDUE IN BREAD BOWLS

Great with a big green salad. More of a meal than a side dish!

> 1 loaf French bread
> 1 garlic bulb
> 6 tablespoons butter
> 7 teaspoons sesame seeds
> 2 cups Monterey Jack cheese, cubed
> 1 1/2 cups sour cream
> 1/4 cup grated Parmesan cheese
> 2 teaspoons lemon pepper
> 2 teaspoons chopped fresh parsley
> 2 cups canned artichoke hearts, rinsed, drained

Cut the bread lengthwise into halves. Tear out chunks from the soft centers of each bread half, leaving the crust intact to form bread shells. Reserve the bread chunks. Place the bread shells upright on a foil-covered baking sheet; set aside.

Separate the garlic bulb into cloves. Peel and finely chop the cloves. Melt the butter in a large skillet over medium heat. Add the garlic and sesame seeds. Cook for 1 to 2 minutes, being careful not to burn the garlic. Stir in the reserved bread chunks. Cook until the bread is lightly browned and the butter is absorbed. Remove from the heat.

Combine the Monterey Jack cheese, sour cream, Parmesan cheese, lemon pepper and parsley in a large bowl. Add the artichoke hearts and bread mixture and mix well. Spoon into the bread shells. Cover with foil.

Bake at 350 degrees for 20 minutes. Uncover the bread shells. Bake for 10 minutes. Let stand for 5 to 8 minutes before cutting.

YIELD: 8 TO 10 SERVINGS

DINNER PARTY DELICACIES

entrées

Our grand homes beg to be utilized
as they were in years gone by,
open to our friends for a formal dinner
party. The beautiful china is the
only appropriate way to
serve the delicious main dish to come.

BEEF TENDERLOIN WITH
MAYTAG BLUE CHEESE SAUCE

BEEF

1 (4-pound) beef tenderloin,
  trimmed
4 garlic cloves, minced
^{1}/3 cup cracked black peppercorns
1 cup soy sauce
^{1}/2 cup Worcestershire sauce
^{1}/4 cup dry sherry
1 cup beef bouillon

SAUCE

4 ounces Maytag blue cheese
^{1}/2 cup (1 stick) unsalted butter
1 tablespoon Worcestershire sauce
^{1}/2 teaspoon caraway seeds
^{1}/2 cup chopped scallions
8 ounces fresh mushrooms, sliced

For the beef, pat the tenderloin dry. Rub the surface with the garlic and press the pepper-corns into the sides. Combine the soy sauce, Worcestershire sauce and sherry in a nonaluminum baking dish. Add the tenderloin. Marinate, covered, in the refrigerator for 8 to 12 hours.

Drain and discard the marinade, leaving the tenderloin in the dish. Pour the bouillon around the beef. Place in a 475-degree oven. Immediately reduce the oven temperature to 325 degrees. Roast for 18 minutes per pound for rare and 20 minutes per pound for medium-rare or until a meat thermometer registers 130 to 140 degrees. Cover the tenderloin with foil. Let stand for 10 to 15 minutes.

For the sauce, combine the blue cheese, butter, Worcestershire sauce and caraway seeds in a heavy saucepan over low heat. Cook until the cheese and butter melt, stirring constantly. Stir in the scallions and mushrooms. Cook for 3 to 4 minutes. Remove from the heat. Slice the tenderloin and serve with the blue cheese sauce.

YIELD: 12 SERVINGS

FILLET OF BEEF IN PHYLLO PASTRY WITH MADEIRA WINE SAUCE

BEEF
3 pounds beef tenderloin, trimmed
Salt
2 tablespoons unsalted butter
8 ounces fresh mushrooms, minced
2 shallots or green onions, minced
1 (16-ounce) package frozen phyllo,
   thawed
$^1/2$ cup (1 stick) butter, melted

MADEIRA WINE SAUCE
3 tablespoons butter
$1^1/2$ tablespoons flour
$^3/4$ cup beef broth
1 teaspoon Kitchen Bouquet
$^1/4$ cup madeira

For the beef, rub the tenderloin with salt. Sear in 2 tablespoons butter in a heavy skillet over high heat until browned on all sides; set aside. Combine the mushrooms and shallots in a bowl. Layer 12 sheets of the phyllo dough, brushing each sheet with melted butter. Spread about $^1/2$ of the mushroom mixture over the phyllo. Place the seared beef in the center of the phyllo. Spread the remaining mushroom mixture over the beef. Fold the phyllo dough around the beef. Layer 5 to 6 sheets of the remaining phyllo dough, brushing each sheet with melted butter. Place over the beef, overlapping with the existing phyllo to seal all the edges. Brush with melted butter. Place the beef in a buttered roasting pan.

Bake at 400 degrees for 40 to 45 minutes or until the pastry is browned and flaky and a meat thermometer registers 135 to 140 degrees.

For the sauce, melt the butter in a saucepan. Stir in the flour. Cook for 5 minutes, stirring constantly. Add the beef broth, Kitchen Bouquet and madeira, stirring constantly. Cook over low heat until thickened, stirring frequently.

To serve, remove the beef to a serving platter. Slice and serve with Madeira Wine Sauce.

YIELD: 10 SERVINGS

BEEF KABOBS WITH HONEY GLAZE MARINADE

2 tablespoons soy sauce
2 tablespoons honey
1 tablespoon grated fresh gingerroot, or 1 teaspoon ground ginger
1 teaspoon grated lemon zest
1 garlic clove, crushed
1/4 teaspoon crushed red pepper
1 (5-pound) sirloin tip roast, cut into 1 1/2-inch cubes
2 red or white onions
1 green bell pepper
1 red bell pepper
1 yellow bell pepper
1 large zucchini
1 pound fresh mushrooms
2 pints cherry tomatoes

Combine the soy sauce, honey, gingerroot, lemon zest, garlic and red pepper in a shallow dish and mix well. Add the beef, stirring to coat with the marinade. Marinate, covered, in the refrigerator for 8 to 12 hours, stirring occasionally.

Cut the onions, bell peppers and zucchini into large chunks for skewering. Remove and discard any large stems from the mushrooms. Remove the beef from the marinade, reserving the marinade. Alternately thread the beef, tomatoes, onions, bell peppers, mushrooms and zucchini on skewers.

Grill over hot coals for 6 minutes, turning often and basting with the reserved marinade during the first 3 minutes only. Discard any remaining marinade.

YIELD: 10 SERVINGS

BAKED VEAL PARMESAN

1/2 cup cornflake crumbs
1/4 cup grated Parmesan cheese
1/2 teaspoon salt
Dash of pepper
2 eggs
4 veal cutlets
1/2 cup (1 stick) butter or margarine
2 (8-ounce) cans tomato sauce
1/4 cup sugar
1/2 teaspoon oregano
Dash of onion salt
1/2 cup shredded mozzarella cheese

Combine the cornflake crumbs, Parmesan cheese, salt and pepper in a shallow dish. Lightly beat the eggs in another shallow dish. Dip the veal cutlets in the eggs and then the crumb mixture to coat. Melt the butter in a 9×13-inch baking dish in a 400-degree oven. Place the cutlets in the dish. Bake at 400 degrees for 20 minutes. Turn the cutlets over. Bake for 20 minutes.

Combine the tomato sauce, sugar, oregano and onion salt in a saucepan. Bring to a boil. Pour over the baked cutlets. Top with the mozzarella cheese. Bake until the cheese melts. Serve over noodles.

YIELD: 4 SERVINGS

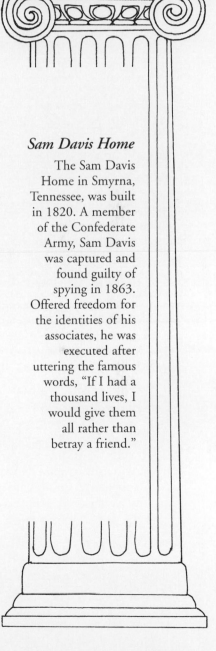

Sam Davis Home

The Sam Davis Home in Smyrna, Tennessee, was built in 1820. A member of the Confederate Army, Sam Davis was captured and found guilty of spying in 1863. Offered freedom for the identities of his associates, he was executed after uttering the famous words, "If I had a thousand lives, I would give them all rather than betray a friend."

GRILLED LAMB CHOPS

8 (5-ounce) lamb chops
1 egg yolk
2 tablespoons white wine
2 tablespoons roasted garlic purée
1/2 cup olive oil
1 1/2 tablespoons chopped fresh rosemary
Salt and pepper to taste

Trim most of the fat from the lamb chops. Arrange the lamb chops in a shallow glass dish. Whisk the egg yolk, wine and garlic purée in a bowl until smooth. Add the olive oil gradually, whisking constantly to form an emulsion. Thin with additional wine if necessary. Stir in the rosemary. Coat the chops with the garlic mixture. Marinate, covered, in the refrigerator for 3 to 12 hours. Bring the chops to room temperature. Season with salt and pepper. Grill for 3 minutes on each side for medium-rare.

YIELD: 4 SERVINGS

PINEAPPLE-GLAZED HAM

1 (10-pound) smoked ham
3 tablespoons whole cloves
1 (20-ounce) can crushed pineapple
2 cups pineapple juice
1 1/2 cups packed brown sugar
1 cup bourbon
1/2 teaspoon salt

Remove and discard the shin and excess fat from the ham. Score the remaining surface fat in a diamond pattern and insert the cloves at 1-inch intervals. Place the ham in a foil-lined roasting pan. Combine the undrained pineapple, pineapple juice, brown sugar, bourbon and salt in a bowl. Pour over the ham. Chill, covered, for 8 hours. Bake the ham at 350 degrees for 2 hours, basting every 30 minutes.

YIELD: 25 SERVINGS

GRILLED QUAIL WITH HERBED CORN BREAD

QUAIL
8 quail, breastbones removed
1/4 cup olive oil
1 teaspoon salt
1 teaspoon freshly ground pepper

CORN BREAD
1 cup flour
1 cup yellow cornmeal
1/4 cup sugar
1 tablespoon baking powder
1/2 teaspoon salt
1 cup heavy cream
2 eggs
1/4 cup each vegetable oil and honey
1 cup chopped fresh herbs (basil,
    rosemary, thyme)

GLAZE
2 cups crème de cassis
1/2 cup sugar
1 tablespoon freshly ground pepper
1 cinnamon stick
2 tablespoons cornstarch
2 tablespoons water

For the quail, rinse the birds with salted water and pat dry with paper towels. Rub each with 1 1/2 teaspoons of the olive oil and season with the salt and pepper. Chill, covered, until ready to grill.

For the corn bread, combine the flour, cornmeal, sugar, baking powder and salt in a bowl. Beat the cream, eggs, oil and honey in another bowl until well mixed. Add to the flour mixture and stir just until moistened. Stir in the herbs. Pour into a greased 9-inch baking pan. Bake at 400 degrees for 20 to 25 minutes or until the bread tests done. Cool slightly.

For the glaze, combine the crème de cassis, sugar, pepper and cinnamon stick in a saucepan. Simmer until reduced by half. Combine the cornstarch and water in a bowl. Stir into the glaze mixture. Simmer until clear and thickened, stirring frequently. Remove from the heat.

To serve, grill the quail for 4 minutes on each side or until the legs move easily when lifted. Drizzle with the glaze and serve with the corn bread.

NOTE: Quail are often sold with the breastbones removed.

YIELD: 8 SERVINGS

CHICKEN MARBELLA

Great for a crowd, this recipe may be prepared up to two days ahead. For the best flavor, serve warm or at room temperature.

10 to 12 chicken breasts, or 4 (2¹/2-pound) chickens, quartered
1 cup pitted prunes
¹/2 cup fresh oregano
¹/2 cup pitted Spanish green olives
¹/2 cup capers, partially drained
¹/2 cup olive oil
¹/2 cup red wine vinegar
6 bay leaves
Coarse salt and freshly ground pepper to taste
1 cup packed brown sugar
1 cup white wine
¹/4 cup flat-leaf parsley leaves, chopped

Combine the chicken, prunes, oregano, olives, capers with liquid, olive oil, vinegar, bay leaves, salt and pepper in a large bowl. Marinate, covered, in the refrigerator for 8 to 12 hours.

Arrange the chicken in a single layer in a roasting pan. Spoon the marinade, prunes, capers and olives evenly over the chicken. Sprinkle with the brown sugar. Pour the wine around the chicken. Bake at 350 degrees for 50 to 60 minutes or until the chicken is cooked through and the juices run clear, basting frequently with the pan juices.

Remove the chicken, prunes, olives and capers to a serving platter with a slotted spoon. Discard the bay leaves. Top with a few spoonfuls of the pan juices and sprinkle with the parsley.

YIELD: 10 SERVINGS

STUFFED CHICKEN BREASTS WITH HERBED PASTA

TOMATO SAUCE
3 garlic cloves, minced
3 tablespoons extra-virgin olive oil
2 (14-ounce) cans Italian-style stewed
    tomatoes, undrained, finely chopped
3 tablespoons vermouth
2 tablespoons minced fresh parsley
1 chicken bouillon cube
1/2 teaspoon basil

CHICKEN
4 boneless skinless chicken breast halves
Salt and pepper to taste
Garlic powder to taste
Flour for coating
2 tablespoons extra-virgin olive oil
1 tablespoon unsalted butter

PESTO
1/2 cup minced fresh parsley
1/4 cup extra-virgin olive oil
1/4 cup (1/2 stick) unsalted butter,
    softened
1/4 cup freshly grated Parmesan cheese
1/4 cup finely ground pecans
1/2 teaspoon basil
1/2 teaspoon marjoram
1/2 teaspoon thyme
1 garlic clove, minced

PASTA
9 ounces fettuccini
2 tablespoons unsalted butter
2 tablespoons chopped fresh parsley
Garlic powder to taste

For the tomato sauce, sauté the garlic in the olive oil in a saucepan. Stir in the tomatoes with liquid, vermouth, parsley, bouillon cube and basil. Bring to a simmer. Simmer for 20 minutes; set aside.

For the pesto, combine the parsley, olive oil, butter, cheese, pecans, basil, marjoram, thyme and garlic in a bowl. Chill, covered, until ready to use.

For the chicken, pound the chicken breasts to a 1/4 inch thickness. Season with salt, pepper and garlic powder. Spoon 1 tablespoon pesto onto each breast half. Roll up and secure with wooden picks. Dredge the stuffed chicken breasts in flour to coat. Heat the olive oil and butter in a skillet. Add the chicken. Cook for 8 minutes or until browned. Cook, covered, for 6 minutes or until the chicken is cooked through; set aside.

For the pasta, cook the fettuccini according to the package directions; drain. Return to the pot. Add the butter, parsley and garlic powder and toss. Serve the chicken over the pasta and top with the tomato sauce.

YIELD: 4 SERVINGS

GRILLED CHICKEN BREASTS WITH BERRY SALSA

SALSA
12 ounces strawberries, coarsely chopped (about 2 cups)
1/2 cup fresh blackberries, halved if large
2 tablespoons sugar
1/3 cup coarsely chopped red bell pepper
3 tablespoons coarsely chopped red onion
1 tablespoon balsamic vinegar
1/4 teaspoon freshly ground black pepper
1/8 teaspoon crushed red pepper
Pinch of salt

CHICKEN
4 boneless skinless chicken breast halves
1/4 teaspoon salt
1/4 teaspoon freshly ground black pepper
1/4 teaspoon crushed red pepper
1 teaspoon extra-virgin olive oil

For the salsa, combine the strawberries and blackberries in a glass bowl. Add the sugar and stir gently. Let stand for 5 minutes. Stir in the bell pepper, onion, vinegar, black pepper, red pepper and salt. Let stand at room temperature for 20 minutes to allow the flavors to blend.

For the chicken, place the chicken breasts in a single layer on a plate. Combine the salt, black pepper and red pepper in a cup. Sprinkle on both sides of the chicken and rub into the surfaces. Drizzle with the olive oil.

Grill or broil the chicken for 5 to 7 minutes on each side or until cooked through. Divide the salsa among 4 plates. Cut the chicken into diagonal slices and arrange over the salsa.

YIELD: 4 SERVINGS

SAFFRON POTATO CRUSTED GROUPER

3 medium russet potatoes, peeled (2¹/₄ pounds)
1 cup skim milk
2 garlic cloves, minced
1 tablespoon chopped fresh chives
1 tablespoon extra-virgin olive oil
1 teaspoon salt
1 teaspoon freshly ground pepper
Pinch of saffron
2 tablespoons extra-virgin olive oil
1 tablespoon balsamic vinegar
¹/₄ teaspoon salt
¹/₄ teaspoon freshly ground pepper
4 plum tomatoes, cut into quarters
6 basil leaves, cut into thin strips
4 (4-ounce) grouper fillets
2 pounds fresh pea pods, lightly steamed

Cut the potatoes into large cubes and place in a medium saucepan of boiling water. Cook, covered, for 10 minutes or until partially cooked. Drain the potatoes and remove from the pan.

Bring the milk to a simmer in the same pan over medium-low heat. Add the potatoes. Cook for 15 minutes or until the potatoes are tender, adding milk to the pan if the potatoes become dry. Add the garlic, chives, 1 tablespoon olive oil, 1 teaspoon salt, 1 teaspoon pepper and saffron. Mash until the potatoes are smooth; set aside.

Combine 2 tablespoons olive oil, vinegar, ¹/₄ teaspoon salt and ¹/₄ teaspoon pepper in a bowl and mix well. Add the tomatoes and basil and stir to coat; set aside.

Spray a 9×13-inch baking dish with nonstick cooking spray. Place the fish fillets in a single layer in the dish. Spoon the mashed potatoes into a pastry bag fitted with a piping tip. Pipe decoratively over the fish fillets. Bake at 350 degrees for 8 minutes or until the fish flakes easily. Place each fillet on a plate. Arrange 4 tomato quarters and ¹/₂ cup pea pods around the fish on each plate.

NOTE: Placing lemon slices in the dish when baking fish helps to eliminate odor.

YIELD: 4 SERVINGS

HICKORY GRILLED POMPANO WITH CITRUS SALSA

1 each medium lemon, lime, navel orange, pink grapefruit and tangerine
³/4 cup light corn syrup
¹/2 cup white vinegar
2 jalapeño chiles, seeded, finely chopped
Salt and pepper to taste
1 red bell pepper, roasted, coarsely chopped
1 yellow bell pepper, roasted, coarsely chopped
1 green bell pepper, roasted, coarsely chopped
¹/2 large red onion, finely chopped
¹/2 bunch green onions, sliced
2 tablespoons cilantro leaves, chopped
6 pompano fillets
Creole seafood seasoning to taste

Remove the zest from the lemon. Mince and set aside. Peel the lemon, lime, orange, grapefruit and tangerine with a sharp paring knife, removing all the peels and white pith. Working over a bowl to catch the juices, cut each fruit into individual segments by slicing down along the membrane on each side of each segment. Remove the citrus segments to another bowl. Pour all of the citrus juices, including any accumulated juices in the bowl of segments, into a medium saucepan. Add the corn syrup and vinegar. Cook over medium heat until the liquid is reduced by ³/4 and coats the back of a spoon. Remove from the heat. Stir in the lemon zest and jalapeño chiles. Season lightly with salt and pepper; set aside to cool.

Combine the citrus liquid, citrus segments, roasted bell peppers, red onion and green onions in a large bowl. Stir in the cilantro and season with salt and pepper; set the citrus salsa aside.

Season the fish fillets with the Creole seasoning. Grill for 2 to 4 minutes on each side or until the fish flakes easily. Serve topped with the citrus salsa.

YIELD: 6 SERVINGS

BAKED SCALLOPS WITH CREAMY GRUYÈRE

1/2 cup fresh bread crumbs
1 tablespoon butter, melted
1 1/2 cups shredded Gruyère cheese
1 cup mayonnaise
1/4 cup dry white wine
1 tablespoon chopped fresh parsley
1 pound sea scallops, cut into quarters
4 tablespoons butter
8 ounces fresh mushrooms, sliced
1/2 cup chopped onion
Paprika

Toss the bread crumbs with 1 tablespoon melted butter in a bowl; set aside.

Combine the cheese, mayonnaise, wine and parsley in a bowl; set aside.

Cook the scallops in 2 tablespoons of the butter in a medium skillet over medium-high heat until tender. Remove from the skillet; drain well.

Cook the mushrooms and onion in the remaining 2 tablespoons butter in the same skillet for 3 minutes. Add to the cheese mixture. Stir in the scallops. Spoon into 6 individual baking shells or dishes. Sprinkle with the bread crumb mixture.

Broil 6 inches from the heat source for 2 to 4 minutes or until lightly browned; do not overbrown. Sprinkle with paprika.

YIELD: 6 SERVINGS

The Tennessee Walking Horse National Celebration

Held every year since 1939 in Shelbyville, Tennessee, the Celebration sells more than 250,000 tickets to people from more than 40 states. The premier event for the Tennessee Walking Horse, it is at this event that the breed's World Grand Champion and 20 World Champions are named. By the end of the 11-day competition, more than $650,000 in prizes and awards are given.

PENNE WITH SAUSAGE IN CREAM SAUCE

1 tablespoon butter
1 tablespoon olive oil
1 medium onion, thinly sliced
3 garlic cloves, minced
1 pound sweet Italian sausage, casings removed
1/2 pound cooked chicken breasts, cut into strips
2/3 cup dry white wine
2 (14-ounce) cans diced tomatoes
1 cup heavy cream
6 tablespoons chopped Italian parsley
Salt and pepper to taste
12 ounces penne
1 cup freshly grated Parmesan cheese

Heat the butter and olive oil in a large skillet over medium-high heat until the butter melts. Add the onion and garlic. Sauté for 7 minutes or until lightly browned. Add the sausage. Cook for 7 minutes or until the sausage is browned, stirring until crumbly; drain. Add the chicken and wine. Boil for 2 minutes or until almost all of the liquid evaporates. Add the undrained tomatoes. Simmer for 3 minutes. Stir in the cream. Simmer for 5 minutes or until the sauce thickens slightly. Stir in 4 tablespoons of the parsley. Season with salt and pepper. Remove from the heat. (Sauce may be prepared 1 day ahead, covered and chilled.)

Cook the penne in a large pot of boiling salted water until tender but still firm; drain. Place in a large bowl.

Bring the sauce to a simmer. Pour over the pasta. Add 3/4 cup of the cheese and toss to coat. Sprinkle with the remaining 1/4 cup cheese and 2 tablespoons parsley.

YIELD: 6 SERVINGS

ROASTED VEGETABLES AND PASTA

Try adding chicken to this recipe. Just marinate and grill the chicken with the veggies.

6 ounces rigatoni
1 envelope onion soup mix
2 tablespoons fresh thyme leaves
1/4 cup olive oil
2 carrots, cut into 1-inch slices
1 medium zucchini, cut into 1-inch slices
1 eggplant, cut into 1-inch slices
8 ounces fresh mushrooms, cut into halves
1/4 cup olive oil
1/4 cup white wine vinegar
1/3 cup pine nuts, toasted
Freshly ground pepper to taste

Cook the rigatoni according to the package directions, omitting the salt; drain. Rinse under cold water; drain. Place in a large bowl; set aside.

Combine the soup mix and thyme in a bowl. Stir in $1/4$ cup olive oil. Add the carrots, zucchini, eggplant and mushrooms; toss to coat. Divide the vegetables between two 10×15-inch baking pans, spreading them out evenly.

Bake at 450 degrees for 15 minutes. Stir the vegetables. Bake for 10 minutes. Add the roasted vegetables to the pasta.

Combine $1/4$ cup olive oil, vinegar and pine nuts. Pour over the pasta and vegetables; toss to coat. Season with pepper.

YIELD: 4 TO 6 SERVINGS

ALFREDO AND ARTICHOKE LASAGNA

2 (10-ounce) packages frozen chopped spinach, thawed, well drained
1¹/2 cups shredded mozzarella cheese
30 ounces ricotta cheese
8 ounces chive-and-onion-flavor soft cream cheese
4 ounces shredded provolone cheese
2 eggs, lightly beaten
1 teaspoon pepper
2 (10-ounce) containers Alfredo sauce
2 (14-ounce) cans artichoke hearts, drained, coarsely chopped
6 ounces shredded Parmesan cheese
¹/4 cup mayonnaise
6 green onions, sliced
12 lasagna noodles, cooked, drained

Combine the spinach, 1 cup of the mozzarella cheese, ricotta cheese, cream cheese, provolone cheese, eggs and pepper in a bowl; set aside.

Combine 1 container Alfredo sauce, the artichokes, Parmesan cheese, mayonnaise and green onions in a bowl; set aside.

Spread the remaining container Alfredo sauce evenly on the bottoms of 2 lightly greased 8-inch square baking dishes. In each dish, layer 2 lasagna noodles and ¹/4 of the spinach mixture. Repeat the layers, ending with the remaining lasagna noodles. Spread ¹/2 of the artichoke mixture over the noodles in each dish.

Bake at 350 degrees for 40 minutes or until just set and lightly browned. Sprinkle the remaining ¹/2 cup mozzarella cheese evenly over the tops. Bake for 5 minutes. Let stand for 15 minutes before serving.

NOTE: May cool the lasagna completely, wrap in heavy-duty foil and freeze for up to 1 month.

YIELD: 8 TO 12 SERVINGS

ITALIAN PASTA BAKE

1¹/2 pounds ground beef
1¹/2 cups tomato sauce
1 teaspoon salt
1 teaspoon sugar
1 teaspoon garlic powder
Oregano to taste
Pepper to taste
6 ounces cream cheese, softened
1 cup sour cream
3 green onions with tops, chopped
10 ounces egg noodles
1¹/2 cups grated Parmesan cheese

Brown the ground beef in a skillet, stirring until crumbly; drain. Add the tomato sauce, salt, sugar, garlic powder, oregano and pepper. Simmer for 30 minutes.

Combine the cream cheese, sour cream and green onions in a bowl; set aside.

Cook the noodles according to the package directions; drain. Layer the noodles, sour cream mixture, tomato sauce and Parmesan cheese ¹/2 at a time in a greased 9×13-inch baking dish. Bake at 350 degrees for 20 minutes or until heated through.

NOTE: May make this a day ahead, cover and refrigerate.

YIELD: 8 SERVINGS

One-to-One Reading

The one-to-one reading program brings one JLM volunteer together with one child for one goal: improving academic achievement through increased reading skill. The JLM member will read with the same child each week for 30 minutes at the school the child attends. This endeavor was an outgrowth of the mentoring project, fostered during Melinda Haines' presidential term.

AFTER DINNER DELIGHTS

desserts

A walk to the parlor helps to create an
appetite for the ending of the meal. Gather
around the piano and enjoy desserts as
only Southern ladies can make them.
Relax; the house will be open for hours.

CRÈME COURVOISIER

1 cup sugar
3/4 cup water
8 egg yolks
1/3 cup Courvoisier Cognac
1 cup whipping cream
Nutmeg

Heat the sugar and water in a 1¹/2-quart saucepan over high heat, stirring until the sugar dissolves. Bring to a boil. Boil for 5 minutes without stirring.

Beat the egg yolks at high speed in a large mixing bowl. Add the hot sugar syrup gradually, beating constantly at high speed until thick and completely cool. Fold in the Cognac gradually; set aside.

Beat the cream in a chilled mixing bowl with chilled beaters until soft peaks form. Fold in about ¹/2 of the egg yolk mixture gently. Add the cream mixture to the remaining egg yolk mixture. Fold in gently. Pour into stemmed glasses if desired. Freeze, covered, for at least 8 hours or until firm. Sprinkle with nutmeg. Serve with pirouette cookies.

NOTE: Must use an electric mixer to beat the egg yolks and cream, not a blender or food processor. To avoid raw eggs that may carry salmonella, we suggest using an equivalent amount of pasteurized egg substitute.

YIELD: 6 TO 8 SERVINGS

RASPBERRY CRÈME BRÛLÉE

48 fresh raspberries
2¹/₂ cups heavy cream
8 egg yolks
¹/₃ cup sugar
Pinch of salt
1 teaspoon vanilla extract
¹/₄ cup sugar

Place 8 raspberries in each of 6 ramekins. Bring the cream to a simmer in a saucepan. Whisk the egg yolks, ¹/₃ cup sugar and salt in a bowl until well blended. Whisk in the hot cream gradually. Stir in the vanilla. Divide evenly among the ramekins. Place in a baking pan. Add boiling water to the pan to come halfway up the sides of the ramekins.

Bake at 300 degrees for 35 to 40 minutes or until set. Do not overbake the custards. Remove from the pan; cool on a wire rack. Refrigerate, covered, until thoroughly chilled.

Just before serving, sprinkle 2 teaspoons sugar over the top of each custard. Broil for a few seconds or until the sugar is lightly browned and caramelized. Garnish with fresh raspberries.

YIELD: 6 SERVINGS

CLASSIC VANILLA FLAN

2 cups whole milk, scalded
3 eggs, lightly beaten
1^1/$_4$ cups sugar
1 teaspoon vanilla extract
^{1}/$_4$ cup water

Beat the milk, eggs, ^{1}/$_2$ cup of the sugar and vanilla in a medium bowl until smooth; set aside.

Heat the remaining ^{3}/$_4$ cup sugar with the water in a small saucepan over medium heat until the sugar crystallizes into hard lumps, stirring constantly. Cook until the sugar melts into a light brown liquid caramel, stirring constantly. Spoon the caramel quickly into 4 to 6 custard cups, coating the bottoms. Let stand until cool. Pour the egg mixture over the cooled caramel. Place the custard cups in a baking pan of shallow water.

Bake at 300 degrees for 1 hour or until a knife inserted into the center of the custards comes out clean. Run a knife around the inside edge of each custard cup. Invert quickly onto serving plates. Serve warm or at room temperature.

YIELD: 4 TO 6 SERVINGS

MOCHA MOUSSE

28 large marshmallows
1 cup strong brewed coffee
1/2 teaspoon almond extract
1 cup whipping cream, whipped
Ladyfingers or angel food cake slices

Place the marshmallows and coffee in a double boiler over simmering water. Heat until the marshmallows melt. Stir in the almond extract. Remove from the heat; cool completely. Fold in the whipped cream. Pour into a bowl lined with ladyfingers or angel food cake slices. Chill, covered, until ready to serve. Garnish with toasted almonds and grated chocolate.

NOTE: This dessert tastes better if prepared the day before serving. May be made up to 3 days ahead, covered and chilled.

YIELD: 8 SERVINGS

The Kleer Vu Restaurant

In 1967, Wilhemina Patterson took over the operation of a small kitchen located in the back room of a Murfreesboro grocery. Today, the landmark serves traditional "Southern cooking" to over 1,500 customers each week. Hot water corn bread is one of their many specialties as well as fried chicken, BBQ pork, and chess pie. The Kleer Vu has had many famous visitors come through its doors, most notably the Pulitzer Prize winning author Alex Haley.

CALIFORNIA CHEESECAKE

CRUST
1 (12-ounce) package vanilla wafers
1/2 cup (1 stick) butter, melted

FILLING
32 ounces cream cheese, softened
2 cups sour cream
4 eggs
1 1/2 cups sugar
1 tablespoon vanilla extract
1 tablespoon lemon juice
1/8 teaspoon salt

For the crust, crush the vanilla wafers into fine crumbs. Combine the crumbs and butter in a bowl. Press onto the bottom and side of a 10-inch springform pan; set aside.

For the filling, beat the cream cheese and sour cream in a bowl. Beat the eggs and sugar in another bowl until thick. Add to the cheese mixture and mix well. Beat in the vanilla, lemon juice and salt. Pour into the prepared crust.

Bake at 375 degrees for 30 minutes. Must cool on a wire rack for 3 hours. Chill, covered, for at least 8 hours before removing the side of the pan and serving.

YIELD: 12 TO 14 SERVINGS

CHOCOLATE CHIP CHEESECAKE

CRUST
2 cups crushed chocolate sandwich cookies
2 tablespoons melted butter

FILLING
3 eggs, beaten
16 ounces cream cheese, softened
3/4 cup sugar
1 teaspoon vanilla extract
1/2 cup whipping cream
1 cup (6 ounces) chocolate chips

GLAZE
1/4 cup chocolate chips
1 teaspoon shortening, melted

For the crust, combine the crushed sandwich cookies and melted butter in a bowl. Press into the bottom of a 10-inch springform pan; set aside.

For the filling, beat the eggs, cream cheese, sugar and vanilla in a large mixing bowl until smooth. Beat in the whipping cream. Stir in the chocolate chips. Pour into the prepared springform pan. Bake at 325 degrees for 1 hour or until set. Remove to a wire rack to cool completely.

For the glaze, add the chocolate chips to the melted shortening in a bowl while still warm. Stir until well blended and the chocolate chips are melted.

Drizzle the glaze over the cooled cheesecake. Chill for 8 to 24 hours before serving.

YIELD: 8 TO 12 SERVINGS

TIRAMISU

16 ounces mascarpone cheese
1¹/4 cups heavy cream
1/4 cup confectioners' sugar
1¹/2 teaspoons vanilla extract
1 cup brewed espresso
1/4 to ¹/2 cup amaretto
2 (3-ounce) packages ladyfingers
4 ounces bittersweet chocolate, grated

Beat the mascarpone cheese, cream, confectioners' sugar and vanilla at high speed in a mixing bowl for 30 seconds or just until blended; set aside. Combine the espresso and amaretto in a bowl.

Layer the ladyfingers, espresso mixture, cheese mixture and grated chocolate ¹/2 at a time in a 3-quart bowl or trifle dish, brushing the ladyfingers with the espresso mixture. Chill, covered, for 8 hours.

VARIATION: For any easy but delicious Toffee Tiramisu, cut one thawed frozen pound cake into 14 slices and halve diagonally. Stir together the espresso mixture. Combine 8 ounces mascarpone cheese, ¹/2 cup confectioners' sugar, ¹/2 cup chocolate syrup and 2¹/2 cups whipped topping in a mixing bowl; beat until fluffy. Layer in a trifle dish as above but use two 1-ounce English toffee candy bars coarsely chopped in place of the bittersweet chocolate.

YIELD: 8 SERVINGS

SNICKERS BAR DELIGHT

Tastes just like a Snickers Bar!

>1 cup (6 ounces) milk chocolate chips
>1/4 cup butterscotch chips
>1/4 cup creamy peanut butter
>1/4 cup (1/2 stick) butter
>1 cup sugar
>1/4 cup evaporated milk
>1 1/2 cups marshmallow creme
>1/4 cup creamy peanut butter
>1 teaspoon vanilla extract
>1 1/2 cups chopped salted peanuts
>1 (14-ounce) package caramels
>1/4 cup heavy cream
>1 cup (6 ounces) milk chocolate chips
>1/4 cup each butterscotch chips and creamy peanut butter

Combine 1 cup chocolate chips, 1/4 cup butterscotch chips and 1/4 cup peanut butter in a small saucepan. Cook over low heat until melted and smooth, stirring constantly. Spread onto the bottom of a greased 9×13-inch baking pan. Chill until set.

Melt the butter in a saucepan over medium-high heat. Add the sugar and evaporated milk. Bring to a boil. Boil for 5 minutes, stirring constantly. Remove from the heat. Add the marshmallow creme, 1/4 cup peanut butter and vanilla and mix well. Stir in the peanuts. Spread over the chocolate mixture. Chill until set.

Combine the caramels and cream in a saucepan. Cook over low heat until the caramels melt and the mixture is smooth, stirring constantly. Spread over the peanut layer. Chill until set.

Combine 1 cup chocolate chips, 1/4 cup butterscotch chips and 1/4 cup peanut butter in a saucepan. Cook over low heat until melted and smooth, stirring constantly. Pour over the caramel layer. Chill for at least 1 hour. Cut into 1-inch squares. Store, covered, in the refrigerator.

NOTE: Lightly spray measuring spoons or cups with nonstick cooking spray before measuring out sticky ingredients such as honey, syrups, molasses or peanut butter.

YIELD: 8 DOZEN BARS

CHOCOLATE TOWER

1 (17-ounce) package fudge brownie mix
2 packages instant chocolate mousse mix
6 (1-ounce) chocolate toffee bars, chopped
16 ounces whipped topping

Prepare the brownie mix according to the package directions; cool completely. Crumble the brownies into a bowl. Prepare the chocolate mousse mix according to the package directions.

Layer the crumbled brownies, chocolate mousse, toffee bars and whipped topping $1/2$ at a time in a trifle dish. Serve immediately or chill, covered, until ready to serve.

YIELD: 10 TO 12 SERVINGS

FROZEN OREO DESSERT

30 Oreo chocolate sandwich cookies, crushed
6 tablespoons margarine, melted
$1/2$ gallon vanilla ice cream, softened
3 ounces semisweet chocolate
2 tablespoons margarine
1 cup evaporated milk
$3/4$ cup sugar

Combine the crushed cookies and 6 tablespoons melted margarine in a bowl. Press into a greased 9×13-inch pan. Freeze, covered, until firm. Spread the softened ice cream over the cookie layer; freeze. Melt the chocolate and 2 tablespoons margarine in a saucepan. Stir in the evaporated milk and sugar. Cook for 8 minutes, stirring frequently. Remove from the heat. Cool completely. Spread over the ice cream layer. Freeze until firm. Cut into 12 pieces to serve. Store, covered, in the freezer.

YIELD: 12 SERVINGS

AFTER DINNER DELIGHTS

ORANGE CHAMPAGNE SORBET

3/4 cup sugar
3/4 cup water
1 cup chilled Champagne
2 tablespoons fresh orange juice
1 egg white

Combine the sugar and water in a small saucepan. Bring to a simmer over medium heat, stirring until the sugar dissolves. Simmer for 10 minutes. Remove from the heat. Chill for about 2 hours.

Combine 1 cup of the sugar syrup, Champagne and orange juice in a bowl. Pour into an ice cream freezer container. Freeze using manufacturer's directions until frozen but still soft. Beat the egg white in a mixing bowl until frothy. Add to the ice cream freezer container. Continue freezing until firm.

NOTE: To avoid raw eggs that may carry salmonella, we suggest using an equivalent amount of pasteurized egg substitute.

YIELD: ABOUT 1 PINT

Cannonsburgh Village

Murfreesboro's Cannonsburgh Village allows the visitor to experience rural Southern life. The village has more than 25 exhibits from the 1800s and 1900s such as an actual toll gate, a one-room schoolhouse, a blacksmith shop, and a museum that renovates and displays agricultural relics from 1850-1950. The world's largest cedar bucket, which traveled to the 1904 St. Louis World's Fair, resides in the village. A local Murfreesboro factory manufactured the bucket.

PEPPERMINT ICE CREAM

1 quart milk
1 pound peppermint candy
1 pint half-and-half
1 pint whipping cream, whipped

Combine the milk and candy in a bowl. Chill, covered for 12 hours. (The candy will dissolve.) Stir the half-and-half and whipped cream into the peppermint mixture. Pour into an ice cream freezer container. Freeze using manufacturer's directions.

YIELD: ABOUT 1 GALLON

VANILLA ICE CREAM

6 egg whites
1 pint whipping cream
6 egg yolks
1¹/₂ cups sugar
2 tablespoons vanilla extract
1 teaspoon salt
2 quarts half-and-half

Beat the egg whites in a mixing bowl until stiff peaks form. Beat the whipping cream in a mixing bowl until soft peaks form. Fold the whipped cream into the egg whites; set aside.

Combine the egg yolks, sugar, vanilla and salt in a bowl. Stir in the half-and-half gradually. Fold in the whipped cream mixture. Pour into an ice cream freezer container. Freeze using manufacturer's directions.

NOTE: To avoid raw eggs that may carry salmonella, we suggest using an equivalent amount of pasteurized egg substitute.

YIELD: 8 TO 10 SERVINGS

AFTER DINNER DELIGHTS

APPLE CRISP

1 (21-ounce) can apple pie filling
1 cup water
³/4 cup sugar
1 tablespoon cinnamon
1 tablespoon flour
3 tablespoons corn syrup
1 (2-layer) yellow cake mix
1 cup (2 sticks) margarine, melted
1 cup chopped nuts (optional)

Pour the pie filling evenly into a greased 9×13-inch baking dish. Pour the water over the pie filling. Combine the sugar, cinnamon and flour in a small bowl and mix well. Sprinkle mixture evenly over the pie filling layer. Pour the corn syrup over the top. Sprinkle the cake mix evenly over the corn syrup layer. Pour the melted butter over the top. Top with the nuts if desired.

Bake at 350 degrees for 45 minutes to 1 hour or until bubbly.

YIELD: 12 TO 15 SERVINGS

HOT CRANBERRY BAKE

4 cups chopped peeled apples
2 cups fresh cranberries
1 1/2 teaspoons lemon juice
1 cup sugar
1 1/3 cups quick-cooking oats
1 cup chopped pecans
1/3 cup packed brown sugar
1/2 cup (1 stick) butter, melted

Layer the apples and cranberries in a lightly greased 2-quart baking dish. Sprinkle the lemon juice and sugar over the fruit; set aside.

Combine the oats, pecans, brown sugar and butter in a bowl, stirring just until the dry ingredients are moistened and the mixture is crumbly. Sprinkle over the fruit.

Bake at 325 degrees for 1 hour. Serve warm with vanilla ice cream.

YIELD: 8 SERVINGS

Self-Esteem Workshop

Working with children and teens in an economically challenged neighborhood, the JLM coordinates a one-day event designed to increase the self-worth of participants. JLM members provide health education, etiquette training, makeover workshops, and job interview training. This service project is an evolution of the Junior League's Health Fair, started during Melinda Haines' presidential term, and has expanded from focusing on at-risk children at one school to include youth from a wider area.

VANILLA NECTARINES

4 nectarines, halved, pitted
1/4 cup water
2 tablespoons sugar
1/2 teaspoon vanilla extract

Place the nectarine halves, cut sides up, in a pie plate or small baking dish. Add the water to the dish. Combine the sugar and vanilla in a small bowl and mix well. Spoon the sugar mixture into the cavity of each nectarine half. Cover the dish tightly with foil.

Bake at 425 degrees for 20 minutes. Uncover the dish. Bake for 15 minutes or until the nectarines are tender and the juices are syrupy. (Add more water during baking if the juices begin to scorch.) Brush the nectarines with some of the syrup from the bottom of the dish. Serve warm or at room temperature.

YIELD: 4 SERVINGS

GRILLED FRUIT KABOBS

2 bananas, cut into chunks
2 kiwifruit, peeled, cut into quarters
12 to 15 whole strawberries
12 to 15 fresh pineapple chunks
2 to 3 tablespoons butter, melted
1 1/2 tablespoons brown sugar
1 1/2 tablespoons lemon juice
1 teaspoon cinnamon

Alternately thread the bananas, kiwifruit, strawberries and pineapple onto 6 skewers; set aside.

Combine the butter, brown sugar, lemon juice and cinnamon in a bowl. Brush over the fruit. Grill over medium-hot coals 2 to 3 minutes or until the fruit is lightly browned. Serve over vanilla ice cream or pound cake.

YIELD: 6 SERVINGS

APRICOT BRANDY POUND CAKE

1 cup (2 sticks) butter or margarine, softened
3 cups sugar
6 eggs
1/2 cup apricot brandy
1 teaspoon vanilla extract
1 teaspoon orange extract
1/2 teaspoon rum flavoring
1/4 teaspoon almond extract
3 cups flour
1/4 teaspoon baking soda
1/4 teaspoon salt
1 cup sour cream

Cream the butter and sugar in a mixing bowl until light and fluffy. Add the eggs 1 at a time, mixing well after each addition. Beat in the brandy, vanilla, orange extract, rum flavoring and almond extract. Whisk the flour, baking soda and salt together. Add to the creamed mixture alternately with the sour cream, mixing well after each addition. Pour into a greased and floured tube pan.

Bake for 1 hour and 25 minutes or until the cake tests done. Cool in the pan for 10 minutes. Remove to a wire rack to cool completely.

YIELD: 16 SERVINGS

THREE-LAYER ITALIAN CREAM CAKE

Doubling the frosting is recommended for this cake. It is so good, you will want to be sure to have plenty!

CAKE
1/2 cup (1 stick) butter, softened
1/2 cup shortening
2 cups sugar
5 egg yolks
2 cups flour
1 teaspoon baking soda
1 cup buttermilk
1 teaspoon vanilla extract
1 (3-ounce) can flaked coconut
1 cup chopped pecans
5 egg whites, stiffly beaten

FROSTING
8 ounces cream cheese, softened
1/4 cup (1/2 stick) margarine, softened
1 (1-pound) package confectioners'
  sugar
1 teaspoon vanilla extract
1 cup chopped pecans

For the cake, cream the butter and shortening in a mixing bowl until light and fluffy. Beat in the sugar. Add the egg yolks and beat well. Whisk the flour and baking soda together. Add to the creamed mixture alternately with the buttermilk, mixing well after each addition. Stir in the vanilla, coconut and pecans. Fold in the beaten egg whites. Pour into 3 greased and floured 8-inch cake pans. Bake at 350 degrees for 25 to 30 minutes or until the cake tests done. Cool in the pan for 10 minutes. Remove to a wire rack to cool completely.

For the frosting, beat the cream cheese and margarine in a mixing bowl until light and fluffy. Add the confectioners' sugar and mix well. Beat in the vanilla. Spread the frosting between the layers and over the top and side of the cooled cake. Sprinkle the top and side with the pecans.

NOTE: Remember, never beat egg whites in a plastic bowl.

YIELD: 10 SERVINGS

LEMON PUDDING CAKE WITH BERRIES

CAKE
3 egg whites
3/4 cup sugar
2 tablespoons butter, melted
1 tablespoon grated lemon zest
3 egg yolks
1 cup buttermilk
1/3 cup lemon juice
1/4 cup flour

SAUCE
2 cups fresh raspberries, or
   1 (10-ounce) package frozen
   raspberries in syrup, thawed
3 tablespoons sugar
1 tablespoon berry-flavor liqueur
   (optional)

For the cake, beat the egg whites at high speed in a deep mixing bowl until foamy. Add 1/4 cup of the sugar gradually, beating until stiff peaks form; set aside. Beat the remaining 1/2 cup sugar, butter, lemon zest and egg yolks at high speed in a mixing bowl until thick and pale yellow. Stir in the buttermilk, lemon juice and flour. Add 1/4 cup of the beaten egg whites and mix well. Fold in the remaining egg whites gently but thoroughly.

Pour the batter into a buttered 5- to 6-cup soufflé or straight-sided baking dish. Place the dish in a larger baking pan that is at least 2 inches deep. Place the pan on the center oven rack. Add boiling water to the larger pan until it reaches the level of the batter in the dish. Bake at 350 degrees for 1 hour or until the top is well browned and the center feels firm when lightly touched.

For the sauce, combine the raspberries, sugar and liqueur in a blender or food processor and process until puréed. Pour the sauce through a fine strainer set over a bowl to remove the seeds, pressing the purée through the strainer.

Serve the pudding cake hot or cold with the raspberry sauce, scooping portions from the bottom of the dish for the pudding sauce that forms.

YIELD: 6 SERVINGS

DECADENT
CHOCOLATE CAKE

1 (2-layer) package devil's food cake mix
1 (14-ounce) can sweetened condensed milk
1 (12-ounce) jar caramel topping
12 ounces whipped topping
1 (10-ounce) package chocolate toffee bits

Prepare the cake mix in a 9×13-inch cake pan according to the package directions; cool completely.

Poke a generous number of holes in the cake with a wooden spoon handle. Pour the sweetened condensed milk and caramel topping over the cake, filling up the holes. The top of the cake should be moist. Frost the cake with a desired amount of the whipped topping and sprinkle with the toffee bits. Chill, covered, for 8 to 12 hours before serving.

YIELD: 12 SERVINGS

Bradley Academy

Originally built in 1811, this school served as a hospital during the Civil War, and later became the first school in Rutherford County for African-Americans. President James K. Polk attended the academy in 1814 and met his wife, Sarah Childress, while he was a student there. The building is featured in the National Register and currently serves as a multi-use cultural and heritage facility.

OLD-FASHIONED FUDGE CAKE

CAKE
1 cup (2 sticks) butter, softened
2 cups sugar
4 eggs
1 cup flour
$^1/_2$ cup baking cocoa
1 cup chopped nuts
1 teaspoon vanilla extract

ICING
$^1/_2$ cup (1 stick) butter
2 tablespoons baking cocoa
3 tablespoons milk
$^1/_2$ teaspoon vanilla extract
$1^3/_4$ to 2 cups confectioners' sugar

For the cake, cream the butter and sugar in a mixing bowl until light and fluffy. Add the eggs 1 at a time, mixing well after each addition. Add the flour and baking cocoa and mix well. Stir in the nuts and vanilla. Pour into a greased and floured 9×13-inch cake pan. Bake at 350 degrees for 30 minutes. Do not overbake. Cool in the pan.

For the icing, melt the butter in a saucepan. Stir in the baking cocoa and milk. Bring to a boil. Remove from the heat. Stir in the vanilla and confectioners' sugar, adding more sugar, if necessary, to make of a spreading consistency. Spread the icing on the top of the cake.

YIELD: 15 SERVINGS

SWEET AND SASSY THREE-LAYER CAKE

CAKE
1 (2-layer) package yellow cake mix
1 (3-ounce) package vanilla instant pudding mix
1 cup sour cream
1/2 cup vegetable oil
3 eggs
4 ounces German's sweet chocolate, grated
1 cup (6 ounces) chocolate chips
1 cup finely chopped pecans (optional)

ICING
8 ounces cream cheese, softened
1/2 cup (1 stick) butter, softened
1 (1-pound) package confectioners' sugar
1 tablespoon vanilla extract

For the cake, beat the cake mix, pudding mix, sour cream, oil and eggs in a mixing bowl until smooth. Fold in the grated chocolate, chocolate chips and pecans. Pour into 3 greased and floured 8-inch cake pans. Bake at 350 degrees for 30 to 40 minutes or until the cake tests done. Cool in the pan for 10 minutes. Remove to a wire rack to cool completely.

For the icing, blend the cream cheese, butter, confectioners' sugar and vanilla in a mixing bowl until smooth. Spread the icing between the layers and over the top and side of the cooled cake. Garnish with pecan halves and maraschino cherries.

NOTE: Solid and liquid fat volumes measure differently. Never substitute one for the other.

YIELD: 12 SERVINGS

SOUTHERN PECAN PIE

1 1/4 cups dark corn syrup
1 cup packed light brown sugar
1/4 cup (1/2 stick) unsalted butter
4 eggs
1 teaspoon vanilla extract
1/4 teaspoon salt
2 1/2 cups pecans, coarsely broken
1 unbaked (9-inch) pie shell

Combine the corn syrup and brown sugar in a 1-quart saucepan. Cook over medium heat until the sugar dissolves, stirring constantly. Bring to a boil. Boil for 2 to 3 minutes. Remove from the heat. Stir in the butter; set aside.

Beat the eggs with a wire whisk or electric mixer in a 2-quart mixing bowl. Pour in the sugar mixture slowly, beating constantly. Stir in the vanilla, salt and pecans. Pour the pecan filling into the pie shell. Place on a baking sheet on the center oven rack.

Bake at 350 degrees for 45 to 50 minutes or until the filling is set. (Cover the edge of the pie crust with foil during baking to prevent overbrowning.)

NOTE: A glass pie plate will hold the heat from your oven longer and continue to brown the sides and bottom of your crust after the pie has been removed from the oven.

YIELD: 8 SERVINGS

CHOCOLATE CHIP PECAN PIE

2 eggs
1 cup sugar
1/2 cup (1 stick) margarine, melted
1 teaspoon vanilla extract
1/4 cup flour
1 cup pecan halves
1 cup (6 ounces) chocolate chips
1 unbaked (9-inch) pie shell

Beat the eggs lightly in a bowl. Add the sugar and margarine gradually, stirring constantly. Blend in the vanilla and flour. Stir in the pecans and chocolate chips. Pour into the pie shell. Bake at 350 degrees for 45 to 50 minutes.

YIELD: 6 SERVINGS

GERMAN CHOCOLATE PIE

1 cup flaked coconut
3/4 cup sugar
3/4 cup evaporated milk
1/2 cup (1 stick) butter, melted
1/2 cup pecans, coarsely chopped
4 ounces German's sweet chocolate, melted
1 egg
1 unbaked (9-inch) pie shell

Combine the coconut, sugar, evaporated milk, butter, pecans, chocolate and egg in a bowl and mix well. Pour into the pie shell. Bake at 325 degrees for 45 minutes.

YIELD: 8 SERVINGS

BANANA BREEZE PIE

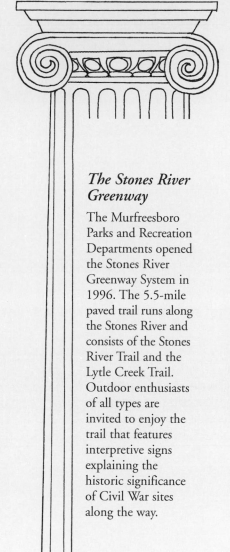

1/3 cup melted margarine
1/4 cup sugar
1/2 teaspoon cinnamon
1 cup crushed cornflakes
8 ounces cream cheese, softened
1 (14-ounce) can sweetened condensed milk
1/3 cup lemon juice
Zest of 1 lemon
1 teaspoon vanilla extract
4 medium bananas
2 tablespoons lemon juice

Heat the margarine, sugar and cinnamon in a small saucepan over low heat until bubbly. Remove from the heat. Stir in the crushed cornflakes. Press into a 9-inch pie plate.

Beat the cream cheese in a mixing bowl until light and fluffy. Add the sweetened condensed milk and beat until well blended and thickened. Stir in 1/3 cup lemon juice, lemon zest and vanilla. Line the crust with 2 sliced bananas. Pour the cream cheese filling over the top. Chill in the refrigerator until firm.

Slice the remaining 2 bananas and dip in 2 tablespoons lemon juice. Arrange on top of the pie immediately before serving.

YIELD: 8 SERVINGS

The Stones River Greenway

The Murfreesboro Parks and Recreation Departments opened the Stones River Greenway System in 1996. The 5.5-mile paved trail runs along the Stones River and consists of the Stones River Trail and the Lytle Creek Trail. Outdoor enthusiasts of all types are invited to enjoy the trail that features interpretive signs explaining the historic significance of Civil War sites along the way.

CARAMELIZED PEAR AND ALMOND TART

1 unbaked (9-inch) pie shell
1 (7-ounce) package almond paste
1/4 cup heavy cream
1/4 cup milk
1 egg
2 egg yolks
1 tablespoon amaretto
3 ripe Bosc pears, peeled, cut into quarters
1/2 cup sugar
1 tablespoon butter
3/4 cup heavy cream
2 tablespoons Calvados

Bake the pie shell at 425 degrees for 10 minutes; cool and set aside. Reduce the oven temperature to 350 degrees.

Combine the almond paste, 1/4 cup cream, milk, egg, egg yolks and amaretto in a food processor and process until smooth. Pour into the pie shell, spreading evenly over the bottom. Bake at 350 degrees for 15 minutes or until set. Cool on a wire rack.

Toss the pears with the sugar in a bowl. Melt the butter in a heavy skillet over high heat. Add the pears. Cook for 7 minutes or until the sugar caramelizes and turns an amber color. Stir in 3/4 cup cream gradually. (The mixture will bubble and turn brown.) Cook until thickened. Add the Calvados. Cook until thickened, shaking the pan and spooning the sauce over the pears occasionally. Remove from the heat. Cool slightly.

Arrange the pears and sauce over the almond filling in the pie shell. Cool slightly and serve.

YIELD: 8 SERVINGS

RASPBERRY ALMOND TARTS

1/2 cup (1 stick) butter, softened
3 ounces cream cheese, softened
1 cup flour
1/3 cup seedless raspberry preserves
1 egg
1/2 cup sugar
1/3 cup almond paste, crumbled
1/3 cup whole blanched almonds, coarsely chopped

Beat the butter and cream cheese in a mixing bowl until light and fluffy. Add the flour and beat until blended. Chill, covered, for 1 hour.

Shape the chilled pastry into twenty-four 1-inch balls. Press over the bottoms and sides of ungreased miniature muffin cups. Spoon 1/2 teaspoon of the preserves into each cup. Combine the egg, sugar and almond paste in a bowl. Spoon 1 teaspoon over the preserves in each cup. Sprinkle with the almonds.

Bake at 325 degrees for 25 to 30 minutes. Cool slightly in the pan. Remove from the cups to a wire rack to cool completely.

NOTE: May freeze the tarts for up to 1 month.

YIELD: 2 DOZEN TARTS

MONSTER COOKIES

1 cup (2 sticks) margarine, melted
3 cups peanut butter
2^1/$_4$ cups packed brown sugar
2 cups sugar
6 eggs
1 teaspoon vanilla extract
4 teaspoons baking soda
9 cups rolled oats
1^1/$_3$ cups chocolate chips
1^1/$_3$ cups "M & M's" Chocolate Candies

Cream the margarine, peanut butter, brown sugar and sugar in a bowl until light and fluffy. Add the eggs and vanilla and mix well. Stir in the baking soda, oats, chocolate chips and chocolate candies.

Drop by rounded tablespoonfuls 2 inches apart on a greased cookie sheet. Bake at 350 degrees for 15 minutes or until lightly browned. Cool on a wire rack.

YIELD: ABOUT 6 DOZEN COOKIES

desserts

LEMON PECAN SANDIES

COOKIES
1 cup (2 sticks) butter, softened
1/2 cup sifted confectioners' sugar
1³/4 cups flour
1/4 cup cornstarch
1/2 cup chopped pecans

ICING
1¹/2 tablespoons butter, softened
1¹/2 cups sifted confectioners' sugar
1¹/2 tablespoons frozen lemonade concentrate

For the cookies, cream the butter and confectioners' sugar in a mixing bowl until light and fluffy. Add the flour and cornstarch and mix well. Shape into 1-inch balls. Roll in the pecans. Place 2 inches apart on an ungreased cookie sheet. Bake at 350 degrees for 8 to 10 minutes. Cool on a wire rack.

For the icing, cream the butter and confectioners' sugar in a mixing bowl until light and fluffy. Add the lemonade concentrate and beat until smooth. Spread over the cooled cookies.

NOTE: To save time when rolling out cookie dough, pat your dough onto a cookie sheet and lightly freeze. Using a pizza cutter, slice the dough into ¹/2-inch squares. Roll individually into balls and place on your cookie sheet.

YIELD: ABOUT 4 DOZEN COOKIES

NO-BAKE COOKIES

1³/4 cups sugar
¹/2 cup milk
¹/2 cup (1 stick) butter or margarine
¹/4 cup baking cocoa
¹/2 cup chunky peanut butter
1 teaspoon vanilla extract
3 cups quick-cooking oats
¹/2 cup raisins (optional)

Combine the sugar, milk, butter and baking cocoa in a saucepan. Bring to a boil. Boil for exactly 1¹/2 minutes. (If undercooked, the cookies will not set. If overcooked, the cookies will be dry and crumbly.) Remove from the heat. Add the peanut butter and vanilla. Stir until the peanut butter melts. Stir in the oats and raisins until well mixed. Drop by teaspoonfuls onto waxed paper. Cool until firm.

YIELD: 3 DOZEN COOKIES

PEANUT BUTTER BLOSSOMS

2¹/4 cups creamy peanut butter
¹/2 cup (1 stick) butter or margarine, softened
1 (1-pound) package confectioners' sugar
3 cups crisp rice cereal, crushed
1 pound chocolate bark

Cream the peanut butter and butter in a mixing bowl until light and fluffy. Add the confectioners' sugar and cereal and mix well. Shape into ¹/2-inch balls.

Place the chocolate in a microwave-safe dish. Microwave on High for 1 minute; stir. Microwave at 10-second intervals until the chocolate is completely melted, stirring every 10 seconds. Dip the balls 1 at a time into the chocolate to coat. Place on waxed paper. Let stand for at least 1 hour or until the chocolate is firm. (If the chocolate becomes too thick, microwave it briefly until thin enough for dipping.)

YIELD: ABOUT 8 DOZEN COOKIES

RASPBERRY BROWNIES

BROWNIES
8 ounces unsweetened chocolate
1 cup (2 sticks) butter
1 cup (2 sticks) margarine
4 cups sugar
8 eggs, beaten
2 cups flour
1 teaspoon salt
2 cups chopped pecans
1¹/₂ cups raspberry preserves

GLAZE
2 cups (12 ounces) chocolate chips
1 cup whipping cream

For the brownies, combine the chocolate, butter and margarine in a microwave-safe bowl. Microwave on Low until melted, stirring every 2 minutes. Beat the sugar and eggs in a mixing bowl until light and fluffy. Stir in the melted chocolate mixture, flour and salt until well blended. Fold in the pecans. Pour into a greased 11×13-inch baking pan. Bake at 350 degrees for 30 minutes or until the brownies test done. Spread with the raspberry preserves. Cool on a wire rack.

For the glaze, melt the chocolate chips in a microwave-safe bowl. Whisk in the whipping cream until smooth.

Drizzle the glaze over the brownies. Cut into squares to serve.

YIELD: 3 TO 4 DOZEN BROWNIES

CHOCOLATE CHESS BROWNIES

1 (2-layer) package chocolate cake mix
1/2 cup (1 stick) butter, softened
1 egg
8 ounces cream cheese, softened
1 (1-pound) package confectioners' sugar
1 teaspoon vanilla extract
1/2 teaspoon almond extract
2 eggs

Combine the cake mix, butter and 1 egg in a large bowl until well blended. Pat into a lightly greased and floured 9×13-inch baking pan.

Beat the cream cheese and confectioners' sugar in a mixing bowl until smooth. Stir in the vanilla and almond extract. Add 2 eggs 1 at a time, mixing well after each addition. Pour over the chocolate layer. Bake at 350 degrees for 40 to 45 minutes. Cool. Cut into squares.

YIELD: ABOUT 2 DOZEN BROWNIES

Oaklands Historic House Museum

Originally built in 1815, the Oaklands Mansion started out as a simple one-story brick home. Built by the Maney family, the house was enlarged as the family prospered and by 1850, the Mansion was the center of a 1,500-acre plantation. As with many historic homes in Murfreesboro, Oaklands was inhabited by the North and the South during the Civil War and still remains one of the most elegant homes in the area.

LEMON COCONUT SQUARES

1¹/2 cups flour
¹/2 cup (1 stick) butter or margarine, softened
¹/4 cup packed brown sugar
1¹/2 cups flaked coconut
1 cup packed brown sugar
1 cup chopped nuts
2 eggs, beaten
2 tablespoons flour
¹/2 teaspoon baking powder
¹/2 teaspoon vanilla extract
¹/4 teaspoon salt
2 cups confectioners' sugar
¹/4 cup (¹/2 stick) butter or margarine, softened
Juice of 2 lemons

Combine 1¹/2 cups flour, ¹/2 cup butter and ¹/4 cup brown sugar in a bowl and mix well. Pat into a greased 9×13-inch baking pan. Bake at 275 degrees for 10 minutes; set aside. Increase the oven temperature to 350 degrees.

Combine the coconut, 1 cup brown sugar, nuts, eggs, 2 tablespoons flour, baking powder, vanilla and salt in a bowl. Spread over the crust. Bake at 350 degrees for 20 minutes. Remove from the oven; cool slightly.

Combine the confectioners' sugar, ¹/4 cup butter and lemon juice in a bowl. Spread over the warm cookies. Cut into small squares.

YIELD: 4 DOZEN SQUARES

OATMEAL CARAMELITAS

2 cups flour
2 cups quick-cooking oats
1¹/2 cups packed brown sugar
1¹/2 cups (3 sticks) butter, melted
1 teaspoon baking soda
¹/2 teaspoon salt
2 cups (12 ounces) semisweet chocolate chips
1 cup chopped pecans
1¹/2 cups caramel topping
6 tablespoons flour

Combine 2 cups flour, oats, brown sugar, butter, baking soda and salt in a bowl until crumbly. Press ¹/2 of the crumb mixture into a greased 10×15-inch baking pan. Bake at 350 degrees for 10 minutes; set aside.

Sprinkle the chocolate chips and pecans over the baked crust. Combine the caramel topping and 6 tablespoons flour in a bowl. Drizzle over the chips and nuts. Top with the remaining crumb mixture.

Bake at 350 degrees for 15 to 20 minutes or until lightly browned. Cool. Chill before cutting into bars.

YIELD: 6 DOZEN BARS

PLAYROOM PARTY

kids' fare

The ladies of Middle Tennessee begin
their entertaining at an early age;
those dolls are smiling for a reason.
They know that the flip side to formality
is fun, and good cooking can begin with
Ladybug Delights and a glass of
Tuity Fruity Punch.

Daffodil Hill

Constructed in 1861 by Confederate Captain Edward Arnold, the home is listed on the National Register of Historic Places. Recently restored and furnished in the correct "period style," the home has had only three owners. When Union soldiers approached the home during the Civil War, Mrs. Arnold was left to defend her home against the soldiers. Evidence of her efforts have been carefully preserved on the steps of the hallway where long Bowie knife marks can still be seen—the Captain's wife slashed at Union officers who threatened to go upstairs to search for her husband.

BANANA PINEAPPLE SLUSHY

2 bananas, cut into chunks
2 cups orange juice
2 cups pineapple chunks (fresh, frozen or canned)
2 tablespoons shredded coconut
5 to 10 ice cubes

Combine the bananas, orange juice, pineapple, coconut and 5 ice cubes in a blender and process until slushy, adding more ice cubes as needed.

YIELD: 6 SERVINGS

TUITY FRUITY PUNCH

3 cups orange juice
1 banana, cut into chunks
2 peaches, peeled, cut into chunks
5 strawberries

Combine the orange juice, banana, peaches and strawberries in a blender and process until smooth.

YIELD: 6 SERVINGS

GOOD MORNING GRANOLA

4 cups rolled oats
1/2 cup wheat germ
1/2 cup slivered almonds
1/2 cup chopped pecans
1/2 cup sunflower seeds
1/2 cup shredded unsweetened coconut
1/4 cup water
1/4 cup vegetable oil
3 tablespoons honey
1/2 teaspoon salt

Combine the oats, wheat germ, almonds, pecans, sunflower seeds, coconut, water, oil, honey and salt in a large bowl with a spoon. Spread on a baking sheet into a thin layer. Bake at 300 degrees until lightly browned and dry to the touch. Stir the granola. Continue baking and stirring at 10-minute intervals until the granola is browned. Cool in the pan on a wire rack. Store in an airtight container.

YIELD: ABOUT 7 CUPS

BANANA OAT WAFFLES

2 cups old-fashioned oats
2 cups water
1/2 banana
2 tablespoons nonfat dry milk powder
2 tablespoons olive oil
1/2 teaspoon salt

Combine the oats, water, banana, milk powder, olive oil and salt in a blender and process until smooth. Let stand for about 2 minutes.

Pour the batter onto a hot waffle iron. Bake until brown using manufacturer's directions. Top with applesauce or your favorite fruit topping.

YIELD: 8 SERVINGS

BREAKFAST CINNAMON PINWHEELS

^{1}/2 cup peanut butter
2 tablespoons honey
^{1}/2 cup soft cream cheese
8 slices soft whole wheat bread, crusts trimmed
2 teaspoons cinnamon

Combine the peanut butter and honey in a bowl. Spread the cream cheese and peanut butter mixture on the bread slices. Lay 2 bread slices side by side with edges touching to form a rectangle. Roll up both slices continuously, starting from a short side, to form a large roll. Wrap in plastic wrap. Repeat with the remaining bread slices to form 4 rolls. Refrigerate for 1 hour.

Unwrap the rolls. Cut crosswise into ^{1}/2-inch slices to form pinwheels. Place, cut sides down, on a baking sheet. Bake at 350 degrees for 10 to 12 minutes or until lightly browned. Sprinkle with the cinnamon.

YIELD: 28 PINWHEELS

COTTAGE CHEESE DIP

2 cups low-fat cottage cheese
1 envelope low-calorie ranch dip mix

Combine the cottage cheese and dip mix in a bowl and mix well. For a smoother dip, beat with a wire whisk or process in a blender. Serve with fresh vegetables.

YIELD: 2 CUPS

PARTY BEAN DIP

1 (16-ounce) can refried beans
2 cups sour cream
1 (16-ounce) jar salsa
1 head lettuce, shredded
4 large tomatoes, diced
2 cups shredded cheese
1 (2-ounce) can sliced black olives, drained

Combine the refried beans and sour cream in a bowl. Spoon onto a serving platter and spread into a smooth flat layer. Top with a thin layer of salsa. Layer the lettuce, tomatoes, cheese and olives over the salsa. Serve with tortilla chips.

YIELD: 32 SERVINGS

NIFTY NACHO CHIPS

3 cups warm water
1 tablespoon salt
10 flour tortillas
Garlic salt or garlic powder to taste

Combine the water and salt in a bowl, stirring to dissolve the salt. Dip each tortilla into the salt water, then place on a paper towel. Cut each tortilla into 4 wedges with kitchen scissors. Arrange the wedges in a single layer on an ungreased baking sheet. Sprinkle with garlic salt.

Bake at 350 degrees for 10 to 12 minutes or until crispy and browned. Serve with your favorite salsa.

YIELD: 40 CHIPS

PIMENTO CHEESE SPREAD

This may be served with crackers or spread on bread for sandwiches. It keeps well in the refrigerator to use as needed.

2 pounds Velveeta cheese, cut into cubes
1^1/$_2$ cups mayonnaise
1 (4-ounce) jar diced pimentos, drained
Coarsely ground pepper to taste

Beat the cheese, mayonnaise, pimentos and pepper in a mixing bowl for 3 or 4 minutes or until fluffy. Chill, covered, until ready to use. Serve with crackers or use as a sandwich spread.

YIELD: 36 SERVINGS

WALDORF CHICKEN SANDWICHES

1 (4-ounce) can chunky chicken spread
3 ounces cream cheese, softened
^{1}/$_2$ medium apple, finely chopped
1 rib celery, finely chopped
2 tablespoons raisins
6 slices whole grain bread

Combine the chicken spread, cream cheese, apple, celery and raisins in a medium bowl and mix well. Chill, covered, for 1 hour to blend flavors. Spread on bread for sandwiches.

YIELD: 3 SERVINGS

KIDS' CLUB SANDWICH

The sauce recipe makes enough for at least 12 sandwiches. This sandwich is served open-face.

SAUCE
1 cup mayonnaise
1/4 cup vegetable oil
1/4 cup chili sauce
1/4 cup ketchup
2 tablespoons lemon juice
1 teaspoon dry mustard
1 teaspoon Worcestershire sauce
1 teaspoon Tabasco sauce
1/2 teaspoon salt
1/2 teaspoon pepper
1/8 teaspoon minced garlic
Grated onion to taste

SANDWICH
Rye bread
Swiss cheese slices
Ham slices
Turkey slices
Lettuce leaves
Tomato slices
Hard-cooked egg slices
Bacon slices, crisp-cooked, crumbled

For the sauce, combine the mayonnaise, oil, chili sauce, ketchup, lemon juice, dry mustard, Worcestershire sauce, Tabasco sauce, salt, pepper, garlic and onion in a bowl. (May be prepared up to 2 days ahead. Chill, covered, until ready to use.)

For the sandwich, layer the bread, cheese, ham, turkey, lettuce, tomato, egg and bacon as for an open-face sandwich. Top with the prepared sauce.

YIELD: 1 SERVING

CONEY DOG SAUCE

8 ounces ground beef
1 (8-ounce) can tomato sauce
1/4 cup water
1/4 cup chopped onion
1 garlic clove, minced
3/4 teaspoon chili powder
1/2 teaspoon salt
1/2 teaspoon MSG
6 bratwurst, cooked

Brown the ground beef in a skillet, stirring until crumbly; drain. Stir in the tomato sauce, water, onion, garlic, chili powder, salt and MSG. Simmer for 30 minutes. Serve over the bratwurst.

NOTE: May substitute kielbasa or hot dogs for the bratwurst.

YIELD: 6 SERVINGS

WHOLE WHEAT BREAD IN A BAG

1¹/₂ cups whole wheat flour
1 envelope dry yeast
1 teaspoon salt
1 cup hot water (120 degrees)
2 tablespoons vegetable oil
2 tablespoons honey
1 cup unbleached all-purpose flour

Place the whole wheat flour, yeast and salt in a gallon-size sealable plastic bag. Seal the bag and shake gently to combine. Add the water, oil and honey. Squeeze the air from the bag and seal. Squeeze the bag until all the ingredients are well mixed. Add the all-purpose flour and seal the bag. Knead the bag until the dough forms a smooth ball. Continue kneading and squeezing the bag for 10 minutes. Place the bag in a warm place and cover it with a towel. Let rise until doubled in bulk.

Punch the dough down. Shape into a loaf. Place in a greased 4×8-inch loaf pan. Let rise, covered, until doubled in bulk. Bake at 350 degrees for 30 to 35 minutes or until the bread tests done.

YIELD: 1 LOAF

CINNAMON PRETZELS

1 (8-count) can biscuits
Brown sugar to taste
Cinnamon to taste

Roll out the biscuit dough into a rectangle. Cut the dough into long flat strips. For each pretzel, twist 2 strips together into a pretzel shape. (May also shape the dough into initials or other designs.) Sprinkle with brown sugar and cinnamon. Place on a baking sheet.

Bake according to the biscuit package directions.

YIELD: 8 PRETZELS

MONKEY BUTTER

1 large or 2 small very ripe bananas
1/2 cup peanut butter
2 tablespoons raisins
1 tablespoon flaked coconut
1/4 teaspoon cinnamon

Mash the banana with the peanut butter in a bowl with a fork. Add the raisins, coconut and cinnamon. Stir until well mixed. Spread on bread.

YIELD: ABOUT 1 CUP

BAKED BANANAS

¹/4 cup sugar
1 teaspoon cinnamon
3 bananas, sliced crosswise
1 cup orange juice
3 tablespoons butterscotch topping

Combine the sugar and cinnamon in a bowl and mix well. Dip the banana slices into the cinnamon-sugar. Place in a baking pan. Combine the orange juice and butterscotch topping in a bowl. Pour over the bananas. Bake at 350 degrees for 20 minutes.

YIELD: 3 SERVINGS

FRIED BANANAS

2 bananas
Flour
Vegetable oil

Cut the bananas lengthwise into halves. Cut each half crosswise to form quarters. Dredge in flour to coat. Pour the oil into a large skillet to a ¹/4-inch depth. Heat until hot. Add the bananas. Fry until browned. Drain on paper towels.

VARIATION: Combine 2 eggs and ¹/4 cup milk in a bowl. Dip the flour-coated banana pieces into the egg mixture. Roll in bread crumbs. Fry as directed above.

YIELD: 2 SERVINGS

LADYBUG DELIGHTS

Chocolate wafer cookies
Red icing
Miniature chocolate chips
"M & M's" Chocolate Candies

Give each child a small paper plate and a dull plastic knife. Place a cookie on each child's plate. Let them spread icing over the surface of the cookies with the plastic knife to form ladybug bodies. Press the chocolate chips on top for the ladybug's spots and 2 chocolate candies on each for the eyes.

YIELD: 1 SERVING PER CHILD

KITTEN COOKIES

White frosting
Chocolate sandwich cookies
Candy corn
Black string licorice
Green "M & M's" Chocolate Candies
Red "M & M's" Chocolate Candies

Give each child a small paper plate and a dull plastic knife. Place a cookie on each child's plate. Let them spread frosting over the surface of the cookies with the plastic knife. Press 2 green chocolate candies on top of each for the eyes and 1 red chocolate candy for the nose. Cut the licorice into 1-inch pieces. Place on either side of the nose for whiskers. Spread a small amount of frosting on the bottom of the candy corn and place 2 on top of each cookie for the ears.

YIELD: 1 SERVING PER CHILD

FIREWORKS FIZZLER

Rainbow sherbet
Cream soda
Candy sprinkles

Give each child a plastic cup and spoon. For each fizzler, place a scoop of sherbet in the cup. Pour cream soda over the sherbet. Top with sprinkles and enjoy!

YIELD: 1 SERVING

PEANUT BUDDY PLAY DOUGH

4 cups confectioners' sugar
4 cups nonfat dry milk powder
3¹/₂ cups creamy peanut butter
3¹/₂ cups corn syrup

Combine the confectioners' sugar, milk powder, peanut butter and corn syrup in a bowl with a spoon. Use as an edible modeling clay. Decorate with assorted candies and sprinkles.

YIELD: ABOUT 12 CUPS

Kindergarten Art Supplies Project

In coordination with local schools, the JLM identifies children who may be unable to afford the school supplies needed at the beginning of the year. Working off the required supply list given by each kindergarten teacher, the JLM ensures that all kindergartners will start the school year with the necessary supplies. This project is traditionally the first "official" service performed by each Junior League member.

KOOL-AID FINGER PAINT

2 cups flour
2 packages unsweetened Kool-Aid drink mix, any flavor
1/2 cup salt
3 cups boiling water
3 tablespoons vegetable oil
Paper

Combine the flour, drink mix, salt, water and oil in a bowl. Let the children use it on paper as a finger paint.

NOTE: This is a nonedible craft.

YIELD: ABOUT 5 CUPS

SILLY FACE AND BODY PAINT

1 teaspoon cornstarch
1/2 teaspoon water
1/2 teaspoon cold cream
2 drops of food coloring

Combine the cornstarch, water, cold cream and food coloring in a small cup. Repeat to make a variety of paint colors. Use as a paint for hands and face. Wash off with soap and water.

NOTE: This is a nonedible craft.

YIELD: VARIABLE

BATHTUB FINGER PAINTS

1/3 cup clear mild liquid dish soap
1 tablespoon cornstarch
Food coloring

Combine the soap and cornstarch in a small bowl until blended. Divide evenly among several sections in a plastic ice cube tray. Add 1 to 2 drops of different food colorings to each section and mix with a small spoon.

Let the kids paint pictures on the inside of the bathtub or use it to play games, such as tic-tac-toe and hangman. The paints may also be used as traditional finger paint.

NOTE: This is a nonedible craft.

YIELD: VARIABLE

SCRATCH AND SNIFF PAINTING

Newspaper
Paper
Watercolor paints
Craft glue
Fruit-flavor gelatin powder

Spread newspaper over the work surface to protect it. Place a sheet of paper over the newspaper. Let the kids use the watercolors to paint a picture of fruit on the paper. Let the pictures dry. Spread glue over the surface of the pictures. Sprinkle gelatin powder over the wet glue. Let the pictures dry again. The glue dries clear, leaving a fruity-smelling picture.

NOTE: This is a nonedible craft.

YIELD: VARIABLE

BUBBLE FLUFF

¹/₂ cup Ivory soap flakes
¹/₂ cup water
Food coloring
Newspaper
Shelf paper or butcher paper

Beat the soap flakes and water in a mixing bowl until a thick and stiff fluff forms. Spoon the fluff into cups or small containers. Stir in food coloring to make desired colors. Cover the work surface with newspaper and lay out sheets of shelf paper or butcher paper. Let the kids apply the bubble fluff to the paper with their fingers. Let the pictures dry for 8 to 12 hours. (Bubble fluff without food coloring resembles snow and creates some neat effects.)

NOTE: This is a nonedible craft.

YIELD: VARIABLE

FLOUR DOUGH SHAPES

1 cup flour
¹/₂ cup salt
¹/₄ cup water
¹/₂ teaspoon vinegar
Few drops of food coloring
Tempera paints (optional)

Combine the flour and salt in a bowl. Add the water, vinegar and food coloring. Mix with your hands to form a dough. Roll out the dough on waxed paper to a ¹/₄-inch thickness. Cut out shapes with cookie cutters. Or, form the dough into shapes as with modeling clay. Place the dough shapes on baking sheets and let them air dry until hard. Decorate with tempera paints if desired. Or store the soft dough in an airtight container to use again.

NOTE: This is a nonedible craft.

YIELD: VARIABLE

SALT GLITTER

¹/₂ cup salt
6 to 7 drops of food coloring

Place the salt in a microwave-safe bowl. Stir in enough food coloring to reach desired shade. Microwave on High for 1 to 2 minutes or until dry. (Or let the salt air dry.) Use in place of regular glitter in craft projects. Store in an airtight container.

NOTE: This is a nonedible craft.

> YIELD: ¹/₂ CUP

SPARKLE BOTTLE

Small, clear plastic soda bottle with cap
Light corn syrup
Assorted metallic confetti
Cold water
Food coloring (optional)

Fill the soda bottle ³/₄ full with corn syrup. Add a small handful of the confetti. Top off the bottle with water. Add a few drops of food coloring. Seal the bottle securely with its cap and shake. The metallic glitter is magically suspended inside the bottle, creating a rainbow of swirling colors.

NOTE: This is a nonedible craft.

> YIELD: 1 BOTTLE

MEASUREMENT EQUIVALENTS

Now that you have all of these great recipes, do you know how to prepare them? In the South, we know that great cooking means knowing what you're doing. Here are some helpful hints to make your cooking great:

A dash	=	less than $1/8$ teaspoon
1 teaspoon	=	$1/3$ tablespoon
3 teaspoons	=	1 tablespoon
$1/2$ tablespoon	=	$1 1/2$ teaspoons
2 tablespoons	=	$1/8$ cup
3 tablespoons	=	$1 1/2$ fluid ounces
4 tablespoons	=	$1/4$ cup or 2 fluid ounces
$5 1/3$ tablespoons	=	$1/3$ cup
8 tablespoons	=	$1/2$ cup or 4 fluid ounces
12 tablespoons	=	$3/4$ cup or 6 fluid ounces
16 tablespoons	=	1 cup or 8 fluid ounces or $1/2$ pint
$1/2$ cup	=	8 tablespoons or 4 fluid ounces
1 cup	=	16 tablespoons or 8 fluid ounces
2 cups	=	1 pint
4 cups	=	1 quart
4 quarts	=	1 gallon

RUTHERF★RD BANK AND TRUST

"Your neighbor is right here."

COOKING TERMS

What does this mean? To enable all of your attempted recipes to be a success we've defined some of the more often used terms in our cookbook:

Blanch—To plunge fruits or vegetables for a short period of time into boiling water to bring out the color or loosen the skin for peeling, then plunge into cold water to stop the cooking process.

Braise—To brown meat in fat over high heat, then cover and cook slowly in the oven in a small amount of liquid.

Cream—To mix a softened ingredient, such as cream cheese, with other ingredients until well blended.

Cube—Cut into 1/2-inch or wider strips; cut across into cubes.

Cut in—Distribute solid fat in dry ingredients by "cutting in" with a pastry blender using a rolling motion or using 2 knives until particles resemble large crumbs.

Dice—Cut into 1/2-inch or narrower strips, cut across into cubes.

Dot—To scatter small pieces of butter over the top layer of a prepared dish.

Dredge—To lightly coat food with bread crumbs or flour.

Fold—To mix one ingredient with another without stirring or beating but by gently lifting from the bottom with a rubber spoon or spatula.

Garnish—To decorate food prior to serving.

Julienne—Stack into thin slices, then cut into matchlike sticks.

Mince—To cut or chop into very fine pieces.

Pare—Cut off outer covering with a knife or vegetable shredder.

Poach—Cook in hot liquid just below the boiling point.

Reduce—To thicken or concentrate a sauce by boiling down, which decreases the volume and intensifies the flavor.

Sauté—Cook rapidly in a small amount of fat, stirring occasionally.

Scald—Heat liquid to just below the boiling point where tiny bubbles form at the edge of the pan.

Sear—To brown the surface of meat very quickly in a pan over high heat to seal in juices.

HERBS AND SPICES

So often we are standing in the kitchen wondering, "What could I do with this food to make it a little different tonight?" Here is a chart of different foods and the herbs and spices that complement and enhance their flavor. Bon appétit!

BEEF

Herbs	Spices
Basil	Allspice
Bay leaf	Chili powder
Caraway	Curry
Cayenne	Onion
Garlic	Orange or
Ginger	lemon zest
Marjoram	Paprika
Mustard	
Oregano	
Parsley	
Rosemary	
Sage	
Thyme	

CHICKEN AND TURKEY

Herbs	Spices
Anise	Cloves
Basil	Curry
Bay leaf	Ginger
Chives	Nutmeg
Dill	Onion
Garlic	Saffron
Marjoram	
Oregano	
Parsley	
Rosemary	
Sage	
Tarragon	

PORK AND LAMB

Herbs	Spices
Anise	Curry
Caraway	Ginger
Garlic	Onion
Marjoram	
Mint	
Parsley	
Rosemary	
Sage	
Thyme	

FISH

Herbs	Spices
Basil	Lemon zest
Chives	Onion
Dill	Saffron
Fennel	
Garlic	
Oregano	
Parsley	
Rosemary	
Savory	
Tarragon	

EGGS

Herbs	Spices
Basil	Onion
Cayenne	Paprika
Chives	Pepper
Savory	
Tarragon	

DRY BEANS

Herbs	Spices
Cumin	Lemon juice
Garlic	Onion
Mint	Saffron
Oregano	
Parsley	
Sage	
Savory	

RICE

Herbs	Spices
Basil	Lemon zest
Fennel	Onion
Parsley	Saffron
Saffron	
Tarragon	
Thyme	

BROCCOLI

Herbs	Spices
Basil	Lemon juice
Dill	Sesame oil
Garlic	Soy sauce
Lemon balm	
Sesame	
Tarragon	
Thyme	

CARROTS

Herbs	Spices
Anise	Ginger
Basil	Honey and
Chives	maple
Dill	Sesame oil
Marjoram	and honey
Mint	
Thyme	

CORN

Herbs	Spices
Chervil	Onion
Chives	Paprika
Garlic	Saffron
Lemon balm	
Pepper	
Thyme	

GREEN BEANS

Herbs	Spices
Basil	Onion
Caraway	Vinegar and
Dill	sugar
Garlic	
Marjoram	
Mint	
Mustard (dry)	
Savory	

MUSHROOMS

Herbs	Spices
Basil	Lemon juice
Coriander	Ginger and
Garlic	rosemary
Marjoram	Paprika and
Oregano	basil or
Rosemary	rosemary
Tarragon	Sherry with
Thyme	onions

PEAS

Herbs	Spices
Caraway	Onions
Chervil	
Chives	
Marjoram	
Mint	
Rosemary	
Thyme	

POTATOES

Herbs	Spices
Basil	Lemon butter
Chives	and pepper
Dill	Onion
Garlic	Saffron
Marjoram	
Parsley	
Rosemary	
Sage	
Thyme	

SPINACH

Herbs	Spices
Basil	Onion
Chervil	Sesame oil
Chives	
Dill	
Garlic	
Rosemary	

SQUASH

Herbs	Spices
Basil	Cinnamon
Dill	Onion
Marjoram	
Rosemary	
Sage	

TOMATOES

Herbs	Spices
Basil	Onion
Bay leaf	
Chives	
Dill	
Oregano	
Parsley	
Sage	
Tarragon	
Thyme	

For a Chinese Flavor: Add Chinese five-spice powder, sesame oil, sherry, or soy sauce. You may also use black bean or hoisin sauce.

For a Creole Flavor: Add bay leaf, Creole seasoning, or Tabasco sauce.

For a Middle Eastern Flavor: Add cinnamon, cloves, curry, or turmeric.

For a Southwestern Flavor: Add chili powder, cumin, or green or red chile sauce.

FOOD AND WINE PAIRINGS

The appropriate wine can enhance your menu and make an evening a success. But what wine goes with what food? The current philosophy has softened somewhat to drink what you like with the food of your choice. However, the right wine can bring out the flavor of food and make a good meal even better. Here are our suggestions:

If eating	Then try**
Salty or spicy, chicken, shrimp, or fish	Champagne or Sparkling Wine
Pastas with a garlic or white cream sauce	Sauvignon Blanc
Rich appetizers, spicy chicken	Riesling
Prime ribs, beef tenderloin, pastas with marinara sauce	Pinot Noir, Burgundy, Chianti
Pot roast, turkey	Shiraz, Zinfandel
Tuna, salmon, duck, rich cheeses	Cabernet Sauvignon, Merlot

If you are mixing food types or are using more unfamiliar foods, try matching the wine with the predominant flavor of your main dish. Here we've matched some of the more common herbs with a complementary wine:

Predominant Flavor	Complementary Wine**
Dill	Sauvignon Blanc, Pinot Noir, Merlot
Rosemary, basil, fennel	Cabernet Sauvignon
Tarragon	Pinot Noir, Merlot, Chardonnay, Sauvignon Blanc
Mint	Cabernet Sauvignon, Shiraz, Pinot Noir, Merlot
Nutmeg, cinnamon	Chenin Blanc, Riesling, Merlot, Shiraz, Zinfandel
Black pepper	Cabernet Sauvignon, Zinfandel, Syrah
Mushroom	Pinot Noir
Soy sauce	Cabernet Sauvignon, Syrah
Butter	Chardonnay
Lemon	Chardonnay, Sauvignon Blanc, Riesling

**A good rule of thumb is to serve white wines slightly chilled and red wines at room temperature.

SERVING COCKTAILS AND WINE

The amount of liquors, mixes, wines, and even ice needed will depend to a great extent on the habits of your guests. These can be used as general guidelines:

	COCKTAILS			WINE AND CHAMPAGNE	
Number of People	*Number of Drinks*	*Quantity Needed*	*Number of People*	*Number of Drinks*	*Quantity Needed**
6	12 to 18	2 fifths	6	12	2 bottles
8	16 to 24	2 fifths	8	16	3 bottles
12	24 to 36	3 fifths	12	24	4 bottles
20	40 to 60	5 fifths	20	40	7 bottles

*How much? We recommend the following formula: Number of persons $\times$ .5 $\times$ number of hours = number of bottles.

How many drinks to pepare per person depends largely on the event. Here are some general guidelines for each person at your event:

For Lunch: 1 mixed drink or glass of wine before lunch, 1 to 2 glasses of wine during lunch, and 1 after-meal drink.

For a Cocktail Party: 1 to 2 mixed drinks or glasses of wine during the first hour, and 2 mixed drinks or glasses of wine per hour thereafter.

For a Dinner Party: 2 mixed drinks or glasses of wine before dinner, 1 to 2 glasses of wine during dinner, and 1 to 2 after-dinner drinks.

A GATHERING OF FRIENDS

We would like to sincerely thank the following people and companies who generously supported The Junior League of Murfreesboro in our *Open House* cookbook project. We are very proud of being able to *strengthen the community, one child at a time,* and your financial gift helps to make it all possible.

VIP GUESTS
Brian and Janet Lee
Murfreesboro Magazine
Rutherford Bank and Trust
The Daily Journal

GRACIOUS GUESTS
First Tennessee Bank
Murfreesboro Medical Clinic
Merrill Lynch—Mitzi Michaelson
Melanie and Barry Shipp

PRIVATE PARTY PATRONS
Drs. James F., Melanie W., and
   James E. Bishop
Gloria and Ted La Roche
Jim and Kristin Ryan
Stones River Total Beverage
TriStar Hospital—Southern Hills

INVITED GUESTS
Sylvia and Milton Beckman—
   Beckman's Prescription Shop
Chip, Karen, Kelsi, Cagney, and
   Carley Carnes
Dr. Donald Bradley, Dr. Joseph Castelli,
   Dr. Brad Chesney, Dr. David
   McKnight, Dr. Gregory Taylor
Lucinda Lea—President 2001–2002
Alexi Lee

CASUAL COMPANY
Elizabeth L. Childress
Cosmetic Dentistry of Murfreesboro—
   Greg and Tonya Nicholson
Anne Courtenay Davis—
   Founding President 1992
Gem in the Box Jewelry Shoppe
Dr. Charles E. Goodman, Jr.
Melinda Haines—President 1994–1996
Jerry and Emily Jackson
Mike, Katie, Nicholas, and
   Elizabeth Jordan
The Kroger Company
Dr. G. William Morton, DDS, and
   Family
Mary Jane Peters
Sloan and Landon Reed
Guy, Elli, and baby Rogers
Suzanne Slayton
Lori Sain Smith
Swain and Company Clothiers—
   David Swain
Bryan and Brayden Terry
Time Frame Custom Framing
Kay Wolohon
Andrew and Leanna Wright

BACK DOOR FRIENDS
BI-LO
Byrn Roberts Inn
Carol and Jeff Clark
Kent and Cecil Coleman
Betty Dixon
Mrs. Jean Alyne Dotson
Durrett Cheese and Gift Gallery
Ken and Lisa Halliburton
Heritage Dairies
Alicia T. Hollis
Eric and Kim Hurst
Ginger Ingle
Pallie Jones
Pam Jones
Judy Myatt
Linda Ranz
Jack and Julia Ryan
Marimae and George White
Tracey K. Youmans

NEXT DOOR NEIGHBORS
Carol Ainsworth
Leslie and Mark Akins
Linda Brantley
In loving memory of Dr. Cliff Gillespie—
    given by Karen and Chip Carnes

Cynthia and Michael Christiansen
City Tile and Floor Covering
The CO-OP Gift Shop
Country Gourmet
Joe and Julie Ennamorato
Jean Farris
Sherwin Harvey
Hastings Books & Music
Heavenly Ham
Lauren Ivey
Brenda Mack McFarlin
Middle Tennessee Board of Realtors
Katherine Ann Minatra
Mary Lane Minatra
Beth Moore
Mrs. Libby Moss
Elizabeth Renegar Parker
Jennifer and Mike Parker
The Peanut Gallery
Ruby's Dress Shop
Salt and Pepper Christian Bookstore
Catherine Stephens
Tag'z Meat Market
Christina W. Taylor
Mrs. Jennifer Timkin
Waite-Taylor Building Group
The Write Impression

OPEN HOUSE CONTRIBUTORS

Just as a successful recipe is a result of the combining of each ingredient, the success of a cookbook is a result of the culmination of the many talents of the people involved. The committee would like to thank the following people who have assisted in the creation of this cookbook. Many gave their recipes, kitchens, and tastebuds. Some gave their time, and some opened their homes to us. The success of our book is the result of each of these people. If we inadvertently left someone out, we sincerely apologize.

Carol Ainsworth
Patty Akin
Leslie Akins
Christie Arney
Rita Ash
Betty Baskin
Shelly Baughman
Sylvia Beckman
Angela Bell
Elizabeth Binkley
Melanie Bishop
Michelle Blaylock
Chontel Bridgeman
Karen Brown
Betsy Bush
Lisa Butler
Colleen Caban
Debbie Caldwell
Jane Campbell
Karen Carnes
Kelsi Carnes
Maureen Caudle
Betty Childress
Julie Clark
Rebecca Climer
Cecil Coleman
Angie Covell
Teresa Craig
Zenobia Craig
Cynthia Christiansen
Amber Culpeper
Patsy Davis

Anne Davis
Lisa DeAugustinis
Eva DenBesten
Melissa Dement
Julie Diliberti
Betty Dixon
Sonya Dodd
Jean Alyne Dotson
Whitney Dotson
Mary Drennan
Laurel Eakes
Julie Ennamorato
Jean Farris
Lesley Ferrell
Melita Fierro
Kyle Flaherty
Sue Flaherty
Corina Flatten
Jessica Florida
Beth Foster
Trish Freely
Laurie Gilley
Peter Goldberger
Laney Golden
Heather Goodman
Delia Goodman
Cori Gorbett
Gwen Greene
Kara Greer
Melinda Haines
Amanda Hales
Sherwin Harvey

Thesa and Denny
   Hastings
LeAnn Hays
Alicia Hollis
Betty Hord
Katherine Hubbard
Debbie Huckabee
Leigh and Bill
   Huddleston
Carol Hudson
Claudia Hunter
Debbie Hunter
Kim Hurst
Ginger Ingle
Anna Ingrum
Lauren Ivey
Emily Jackson
Priscilla Jackson
Terra Jackson
Lynn Jacobs
Sheri Jernigan
Katie Johnston
Janet Jones
Pallie Jones
Pam Jones
Tracy Jones
Katie Jordan
Shannon Kaprive
Joan Kellerman
Laurie Knowles
Gloria LaRoche
Shirley LaRoche

Lucinda Lea
Janet Lee
Christi Leskinen
Christine Lombardi
Beth Loughry
Christy Lovinski
Tara MacDougall
Patty Marschel
Claire Maxwell
Sheila McArdle
Wendy McCarter
Sonya McCravy
Staci McCreary
Rachel McElhaney
Brenda McFarlin
Glenda McKinney
Charlotte McKnight
Kirby McNabb
Mitzi and Rick
    Michaelson
Beth Minatra
Mary Dodd Mifflin
Beth Moore
Tracey Moore-Robison
Tami Morton
Libby Moss
Susan Moss
Betsy Murfree
Kathy Murphy
Judy Myatt
Tonya Nicholson
Cynthia Nobers
Christina O'Neill
Patrick O'Neill
Caroline Ott
Beth Parker
Jennifer Parker
Patty Pearson
Julie Peppers

Mary Jane Peters
Lori Petrilli
Karen Pfeifer
Anita and Mark Pirtle
Gina Poff
Janet Powell
Susan Quesenberry
Nancy Rainier
Holly Ray
Sandy Reed
Amanda Reeves
Liz Rhea
Marchella Richardson
Dana Rivait
Marcella Rodgers
Tonja Rodgers
Jana Rogers
Jennifer Rutherford
Kristin Ryan
Pat Ryan
Carrie Sanders
Doris Sawyer
Olivia Schade
Donna Scott
Tanya Scroggins
Christine Seshul
Michelle Sesler
Pama Sevier
Nancy Shawver
Tabatha Shea
Melanie Shipp
Dana Skidmore
Ken Skidmore
Marla Skipper
Suzanne Slayton
Anita Smith
Lori Smith
Linda Stacy
Katherine Steele

Catherine Stephens
Barbara Sullivan
Lynne Swafford
Heather Sweeney
Lisa Sweeney
Lorenda Sweeney
Linda Tackett
Christina Taylor
Joyce Taylor
Mollie Taylor
Shonn Taylor
Cheryl Terry
Amanda Thompson
Jennifer Timken
Ginny Togrye
Aleta Tuma
Carolyn Tumbleson
Stephanie Turley
Karen VanDerSpuy
Janice Walls
Cindy White
Dawn White
Marimae White
Connie Wiel
Gina Wiser
Lori Williams
Polly Winecoff
Kay Wolohon
Sarah Woods
Leanna Wright
Lisa Yenzer
Tracey Youmans

INDEX

OPEN *house*

A Culinary Tour

The Junior League of Murfreesboro
P.O. Box 4138
Murfreesboro, Tennessee 37133
615-848-0901
www.JLMurfreesboro.org

YOUR ORDER	QUANTITY	TOTAL
Open House at $24.95 per book		$
Tennessee residents add $2.50 sales tax per book		$
Postage and handling at $4.00 for first book; Add $2.00 for each additional book to same address		$
	TOTAL	$

Make check payable to The Junior League of Murfreesboro.

Name

Address

City   State   Zip

Telephone   Fax   Email

Photocopies will be accepted.